ITALIAN COOKBOOK THE COMPLETE GUIDE

DISCOVER THE MOST FAMOUS AND TASTY RECIPES OF ITALIAN COOKING AND HOW TO MAKE THEM EASILY AT YOUR HOME. PASTA, PIZZA, MEAT, FISH, AND MUCH MORE

Olivia Rossi

TABLE OF CONTENTS

INTRODUCTION

*I*talian cuisine is one of the most popular in the world, which you will find served not only in restaurants but also cooked at home. No matter where you come from, you are most likely familiar with Italian dishes such as pizza, spaghetti Bolognese, or tortellini, among others. However, more dishes complement superb Italian cuisine such as meat, desserts, and soups.

Italian food is basically happy food. The recipes in the Essential Italian Cookbook are meant to be enjoyed. From incredible pasta to the smoothest of Tiramisu for dessert, it's all about satisfying the taste buds. Being surrounded by the Mediterranean, Italy also has some delicious seafood. Check them out in this cookbook.

With the many great ingredients from around the world in today's markets, this is a great time to start experimenting with them in the kitchen. Healthy food choices are highly available along with a variety of flavors to please everyone's taste buds. This is all thanks to globalization.

Most of the dishes in the Essential Italian Cookbook are prepared in a simple way. Some meat, some pasta, sprinkle on some herbs, and you have yourself a great meal.

Serve your family some more. Serve them some Italian specialties.

One of the best characteristics of Italian food is simplicity.

It is the combination of fresh ingredients and spices that are delicately seasoned to produce rich flavors.

At the heart of most Italian dishes is olive oil, tomato, basil, oregano, capers, parsley, garlic, meat or seafood, and cheese.

And don't forget the wine.

If there is something you can expect in an Italian family dinner, it's water, bread, and wine.

Most of their dishes only have a few main ingredients that will vary depending on the region.

Northern Italy cooks mostly with fish, seafood, sausages, and pork.

The North is known for its risotto (rice cooked in broth or stock), polenta (boiled cornmeal), and Parmigiano-Reggiano dubbed as "the King of Cheeses".

Central Italy focuses more on tomatoes, meats, bread, and vegetables.

Finally, Italy's southern region use dried pasta, seafood, and olive oil.

South Italy is known for its pizza Margherita, spaghetti alle vongole, and Italian wedding soup.

In this book, we focus on Italian. You will find that even though the recipes are simple, the taste of the dishes is quite amazing.

Italian recipes are some of the simplest recipes to prepare, so even if you're a newbie at cooking, you will be able to cook the recipes in this book with success. If Italian cooking is completely new to you, you will do well to learn about some of the popular ingredients and cooking techniques before we jump into the recipes. The following sections do exactly that.

This cookbook consists of recipes that are easy to make, healthy but also tasty. All recipes are either made with very few ingredients or are very easy to make. In some cases, where cooking with a slow cooker is suggested, cooking time is a bit longer, but recipes are still simple and delicious.

The Italian dishes in this cookbook consist mainly of wheat products, such as pasta and bread, vegetables, meat cheese, and fish. Most of the ingredients used can be found in any country. Apart from adjustments related to ingredients, I tried to use the simplest forms of cooking techniques such as boiling, pan-frying, browning, roasting, baking, and grilling.

This cookbook is arranged in sections ranging from breakfast, seafood, meat, desserts, appetizers and dips, risotto, salads, and soups. The selected recipes are mostly modern takes on traditional dishes or something that you can eat in beautiful Italian restaurants in this amazing country. Are you ready to be transported to the different regions and experience the culinary diversity of Italy?

Let's get started then!

CHAPTER 1

Introduction to Italian cooking

The Cooking of Italy

Italian cooking isn't one specific type of cooking. It's not just pasta and sauce, nor is it just one style of cuisine. The recipes vary from region to region, although the basic ingredients may be similar.

Several factors combine to create unique, distinctive styles of cooking that are predominant in the various regions of Italy. Geography, history, and the economy have helped to shape regional cuisine, and conquering countries have influenced the culture and cooking of the different regions.

Regions in northern Italy had plentiful natural resources. Their proximity to France and Austria and a thriving economy encouraged the development of a diverse and light cuisine compared to the southern regions. The subtlety of flavors, the delicate use of herbs like sage and rosemary, and the modest use of tomato-based sauces are typical for the regions of northern Italy.

The southern regional cooking of Italy is flavored with olives, garlic, basil, and oregano. The trademark tomato is ever-present as an ingredient and the basis of sauces. The cuisine of the southern regions reflects the Greek heritage and Arab occupation influences Sicilian cooking with the absence of pork and the popularity of stuffed meats and vegetables.

These influences, along with the use of seasonal ingredients, produce cuisine that emphasizes fresh ingredients, careful preparation, and maintaining the individual flavors of those ingredients. Know the ingredients:

Fruits and Vegetables

Vegetables and legumes are easily one of the most important ingredients in Italian cuisine. Vegetables and legumes might not be the first things to come to mind when you think of Italian food, but they are responsible for most of the flavor and color of Italian food.

Fruits are naturally sweet and are an indispensable part of Italian desserts, and many other dishes. Make sure the fruit is fresh and ripe before you use them in a recipe. Fruits that are in season are preferred.

Fruits and vegetables should be thoroughly washed before use and used immediately after cutting. If you have to store them, store them properly. Depending on the fruit or vegetable, there is an ideal way to store it. For example, onions and potatoes should be stored in cool, dark places. Broccoli and spinach should always be refrigerated. The best way to store fresh herbs is in a damp towel, or a container filled with water.

Almonds

Almonds are a staple in the Italian pantry and a common ingredient in some of the most popular Italian recipes and desserts. Sicily is revered for its almonds and its almond dishes.

Apples

Italians love to eat apples raw, and also use them in desserts and salads. Applesauce is a great ingredient for low-fat baking.

Artichokes

Italy is the biggest producer and exporter of artichokes in the world, and artichokes are an indispensable part of Italian cuisine. These are used in all kinds of Italian recipes.

Arugula

Arugula is a flavorful, peppery salad green of the mustard family that is an important ingredient in Italian cuisine and grows wild all over the Mediterranean. It is a popular ingredient in salads, sandwiches, frittatas, sauces, etc.

Asparagus

Green asparagus is the most common kind used in Italian cuisine. If you can't find it, white or purple asparagus will do just fine.

Beets

Beets are in season from March to October, so it is best to cook recipes calling for beets during this time. These are vital ingredients for risotto, salads, soups, etc.

Bell Peppers

Peppers come in all shapes, sizes, and tastes. When it comes to Italian cooking, we mostly use the sweet kinds of bell peppers. Sweet bell peppers also come in multiple colors, but all colors taste pretty much the same. As a general rule, the brighter colored bell peppers are sweeter. When buying these, make sure you buy fresh ones with tight skin. Never pick shriveled ones.

Broccoli

In Italian, the word broccoli stands for "cabbage sprout." This is a highly popular ingredient all over the world and needs no introduction. When buying broccoli, check to make sure there are no yellowish buds on it, as this means the broccoli is past its prime.

Broccoli Rabe

Called rapini in Italy, broccoli rabe is an Italian staple and cooked in multiple ways. Most commonly, it is used in vegetable sides, appetizers, pasta dressings, and sandwiches.

Brussels Sprouts

If handled and cooked right, brussels sprouts greatly enhance the flavor of food, and are a common ingredient in Italian cuisine. These go great on the side with Italian meat dishes. Buy them fresh and firm, when they are still bright green in color.

Cabbage

Cabbage is a common ingredient in Italian salads, sauerkraut, pasta sauces, etc. It is insanely nutritious and if cooked right, insanely delicious too.

Capers

Caperberries are crunchy, acidic, and have a strong flavor. They are a common ingredient in Italian antipasto, salads, sauces, etc.

Cardoons

Cardoons are well known in all parts of the world, but they are absolutely indispensable for Italian cooking. These take some patience to work with, but the result is worth it.

Carrots

Carrots are a common ingredient in Italian recipes. They are commonly used in soups and are also enjoyed boiled, raw, fried, or puréed. Always buy fresh organic carrots with the greens still attached to them so you get an idea of how fresh they are.

Cauliflower

Commonly enjoyed raw in Italian salads, cauliflower is commonly cooked by steaming, baking, blanching, or sautéing. Make sure you buy it fresh, without any yellow spots. It is mostly tasteless and super nutritious.

Celery

This cheap and delicious vegetable is one of the most underrated vegetables out there. It is commonly used in Italian soups and meaty salads.

Celery Root

This root is peeled and used in Italian salads, stews, etc. It tastes great when mashed with potatoes.

Cherries

A common ingredient in Italian recipes, cherries are nutritious and loaded with vitamins. They have anti-inflammatory properties too! They come in wide varieties of sweetness and color.

Chickpeas

Also known as garbanzo beans, chickpeas are commonly grown in Southern parts of Italy and are a staple in the Italian kitchen. They are enjoyed making pasta sauces and soups. Chickpea flour is a common ingredient for breads and pastries. They are inexpensive, and great for health!

Cranberries

Although these are not common in classic Italian recipes, cranberries are only now gaining popularity in Italy. This versatile ingredient is now being used by cooks all over Italy.

Edible Flowers

Quite a few vegetables we eat today are actually edible flowers. Artichokes are a great example of this, although they don't really seem like flowers. However, there are flowers like viola that seem like flowers, and can be eaten directly too! Quite a few Italian cooks use these flowers for garnishing, and most people don't eat these, for most people aren't used to eating flowers. These flowers make for a great garnish, just make sure they are free of pesticides, or you can even grow your own!

Eggplant

Eggplants are available in a wide spectrum of shapes and sizes. The eggplant used in Italian cuisine is usually dark purple and evenly elongated. When buying this, make sure the skin is smooth, tight, and shiny. Poached eggplant is a common ingredient, and to poach it, you need to cut the eggplant in sections along the length and poach it in a liquid that is ¾ water and ¼ red wine vinegar.

Escarole

Part of the endive family, escarole is in season during the cold months. The center leaves are light green in color and soft and go great in salads. The outer tougher leaves are usually eaten sautéed or braised with oil and garlic or used in soups.

Fava Beans

When buying these, make sure they are firm, containing fully ripe beans, and with little to no discoloration. If you don't want to go through the hassle of shelling them, you can buy shelled beans from the market, for a bit more money.

Fennel

This vegetable is crispy when raw, and soft and sweet when braised or roasted. It is a common herb in classic Italian recipes.

Fiddlehead Ferns

These are highly seasonal, and a common ingredient in pesto, risotto, morels, etc.

Fresh Beans

Dried beans do the job and are available throughout the year. However, when the beans are in season, they can be obtained fresh, and are used to make some insanely delicious Italian recipes.

Garlic

Italian recipes have always contained garlic, but after being influenced by American recipes, garlic is an even more dominant presence.

Green Beans

Green beans come in hundreds of varieties, each with a different shape, size, and taste. A huge variety of these is used in Italian recipes, and hence are an important part of the Italian pantry. They are diverse and used in a wide array of Italian recipes.

Kale

Kale is an insanely delicious and nutritious winter vegetable. It is a strong antioxidant and anti-inflammatory agent. It is easy to cook, and used in soups, vegetable dishes, and pasta condiments.

Leeks

Leeks belong to the onion family and are usually sweet and mellow compared to yellow and Spanish onions. These make great side dishes and appetizers.

Lemons

There is no limit to what you can do with lemons, and Italian cooking uses them in a wide variety of recipes. If you want to go for authenticity, get the Sorrento lemon variety, which is an Italian favorite. In a pinch, any kind of lemon will do.

Lentils

These dried seeds are nutritious and delicious, and used in all kinds of Italian recipes!

Mushrooms/Wild Mushrooms

Buy fresh and firm mushrooms always. Don't soak them in water for too long, and give them a quick rinse if they are dirty. Preparing them is quite simple too, just chop off any rigid parts before cooking. The white domestically cultivated mushrooms commonly available on the market will do the job, but if you can, try to get your hands on porcini, chanterelles, morels, or wild varieties.

Nettles

These require some delicate handling due to the needle-like fibers on them. However, if you can get past that minor inconvenience, the reward is totally worth it.

Onions

Onions are a staple food from pretty much every country, and Italian food is no exception. Pretty much all kinds of onions are used in Italian cooking, and the kind of onion used may change with the kind of recipe being cooked. Most recipes specify the kind of onion used, but if not mentioned, use the common yellow onions.

Oranges

Oranges are one of the most common fruits available all over the world, and Italy is no exception. This acidic citrus fruit is used in a wide array of Italian recipes and drinks.

Peas

Peas are insanely nutritious, and a staple in the Italian kitchen. Make sure you buy these while they are still fresh and firm.

Potatoes

One of the cheapest and tastiest food available all over the world, potatoes hold an important place in Italian cooking. Potatoes are available in many varieties, and almost all these varieties are used in Italian recipes.

Prunes

Used to cook sweet and savory Italian recipes, prunes are extremely popular in Italy in dried form.

Radicchio

Tasting sweet and bitter simultaneously, radicchio is a common ingredient in Italian salads, sauces, risotto, and much more!

Raisins

Dehydrated grapes are a common ingredient all over the world, and Italy is no exception. These can be reconstituted by soaking them in water. If you want to get creative, try soaking them in other liquids. Rum works great if you're thinking of baking them!

Ramps

Also called wild leeks, ramps have a garlicky sweet flavor, and are used in a wide variety of Italian recipes. They are in season during spring, so make sure you make the most of the season!

Rhubarb

Perfect for making chutneys and some sweet dishes like pies, rhubarb imparts a tarty and fruity flavor to the recipes it is used in.

Romaine Lettuce

Not a traditional ingredient, romaine lettuce is a comparatively modern addition to the Italian cuisine. This long-leaf lettuce is crunchy and soft at the same time.

Scallions

Also known as green onions or spring onions, scallions are a part of the onion family and a common ingredient in Italian recipes.

Strawberries

When strawberries are in season, make sure you cook a lot of Italian recipes that call for them!

Swiss Chard

A taller and larger version of spinach, swiss chard is insanely nutritious and used in a wide array of Italian recipes.

Tomatoes

Tomatoes are used in pretty much every Italian recipe. I can write a whole book about Italian recipes using tomato. A few of the common Italian tomatoes are the Pomodorino del Piennolo, Roma, San Marzano, and the Costoluto Genovese. Tomatoes are mostly used crushed or made into a paste.

Truffles

Truffles can be costly but are totally worth it. They have a strong, distinct aroma and are used in quite a few Italian recipes

Turnips

Turnips are delicious and nutritious and play an important role in Italian cooking. Turnips can be cooked in a variety of ways and are hence used in a wide spectrum of recipes.

Winter Squash

Winter Squash is slowly gaining popularity in Italian cuisine and is used in quite a few Italian recipes these days.

Zucchini

These are cheap, and easily available all over the world. Zucchini is used in all kinds of Italian recipes and should be a staple in the pantry of anyone looking to cook Italian food.

Useful Cooking Techniques for Vegetables

Vegetables are the most important ingredient in Italian cooking, and there are a few cooking techniques you will be using a lot when cooking vegetables the Italian way. Always buy fresh vegetables that are in season, and always check for blemishes. There is an ideal way to store every vegetable. Google it if you're unsure of how to store a particular vegetable you wish to store. Let us now look at some of the commonly used techniques in a little more detail.

Blanching Vegetables

Here's how you blanch vegetables:

Quickly boil the vegetables.

Drain.

Toss with medium-coarse salt while still scorching hot.

Toss them into ice water to stop from cooking further. (not necessary)

With this simple process the vegetables retain their color, texture, nutrients, and taste. You can blanch them in salted water, but plain water is preferable. You can always salt them after boiling.

Grilling Vegetables

Here's how you grill vegetables:

Chop up the vegetable you wish to grill into equally sized pieces, so they finish cooking at the same time. Small pieces cook faster.

Clean the grilling surface and lightly coat it with oil to prevent sticking.

Brush the seasoning and oil onto the vegetables.

Wrap the vegetables in heavy-duty foil and grill.

Take the vegetables off the grill before they become too soft.

Allow them to stay in the foil for a while longer, as they continue to cook during this time.

The time you will need to cook them for will vary with the kind of vegetable. If you're new to this process, you might overcook or undercook them, but you will get used to the timing eventually.

Roasting Vegetables

Some vegetables like squashes, peppers, tomatoes, eggplants, etc. taste great roasted. Roasting greatly enhances the flavor of the vegetable. Here's how it is done:

Preheat your oven to 400 degrees.

Chop the vegetables as you wish.

Coat a baking sheet with parchment paper and lay the chopped vegetables on the sheet.

Season with salt, pepper, and other herbs to taste.

Roast in oven until fairly shriveled and caramelized on all sides.

Sautéing Vegetables

You can do this directly or blanch the vegetables before you sauté. Here's how it is done.

Chop up the vegetables into equal-sized pieces.

Take a frying pan and put some olive oil and garlic into them.

Turn on the heat, and once the oil is hot, throw the vegetable pieces into the pan.

Sprinkle with seasoning and stir/toss intermittently until cooked.

Herbs, Spices, and Seasonings

Herbs, spices, and seasonings should be a staple in every kitchen, Italian or not. But when it comes to Italian cooking, they are absolutely indispensable. If you wish to cook Italian recipes on a regular basis, you will do well to stock your kitchen up with the following:

- Basil
- Bay leaves
- Cinnamon
- Cloves
- Marjoram
- Mint
- Nutmeg
- Oregano
- Parsley
- Peperoncino/crushed red pepper
- Peppercorns
- Rosemary
- Saffron
- Sage
- Salt
- Sugar
- Thyme

Olive Oil, Vinegar, and Condiments

Olive oil and vinegar are indispensable for your pantry if you wish to cook Italian food. Both these ingredients are usually used uncooked, especially when used as dressings. A wide variety of olives are grown all over Italy, and this leads to a wide variety of olive oils too. Below, we will take a detailed look at these ingredients.

Olive Oil

Olive oils are also categorized on the basis of region, but in most cases, any old olive oil you can get your hands on will get the job done.

Olive oil is an Italian staple, and highly nutritious. It is a strong antioxidant. Extra-virgin olive oil is best when used raw, right out of the bottle, to sprinkle on salads and before you serve soup or pasta.

With so many brands of olive oil available today, testing them to identify the best one is a good way to go.

The first thing to check is color. Riper olives usually make yellowish olive oil, while younger olives make a greener olive oil which also has a stronger flavor. If the oil is freshly pressed, it has a very prominent green color. As it ages, the prominence of green weakens.

The next thing to do is to smell it. It should smell fresh, and then taste it. The taste should match the smell and should not feel heavy or greasy in the mouth.

Garlic-Infused Oil

This is a handy little oil to have in your pantry if you wish to cook Italian food on a regular basis. You can make your own by putting three finely chopped slices of garlic for each cup of EVOO. Strain, pout into an airtight bottle, and store in your fridge.

Holy Oil

This is a southern Italian specialty, also called Olio Santo. This oil is spicy and hot, and a great addition to recipes if you like your recipes hot. Here's how you make it:

Pour a cup of good-quality extra-virgin olive oil into a glass jar and drop in a teaspoon of kosher salt and two tablespoons of small, whole dried pepperoncini, approximately ten little peppers.

Cover firmly, and let the oil infuse at room temperature for a minimum of two days.

Shake thoroughly, and use. Store in a sealed jar, in a cool place, for at least one month.

Uncooked Olive Oil Sauce

A quick and delicious sauce that makes for a spectacular dressing. Making this is really simple: all you require is good-quality olive oil, garlic cloves, hot pepper, fresh herbs of your choice, nuts of your choice, and whatever else you want to put in there.

Crush the ingredients using a mortar and pestle and you're done.

Vinegar

Vinegar is another ingredient you should always have on hand if you wish to cook Italian recipes on a regular basis. There are all kinds of vinegar made from all kinds of fruits, vegetables, nuts, grains, etc. When it comes to Italian cooking, some of the popular kinds of vinegar are red and white wine, apple, balsamic, and Saba vinegar. Below are two of the labels to watch for:

Aceto Balsamico Tradizionale

A classic balsamic vinegar made using a traditional method of production, which involves seven years in wooden barrels of different sizes and types of woods. The vinegar so labeled is far superior and is quite costly too. Aceto Balsamico Tradizionale is perfect when used without cooking; sprinkle it on grilled steaks, salads, cheeses, fruit, ice cream, etc.

Aceto Balsamico Commerciale

This vinegar is a mix of the vinegar we talked about above, and vinegar aged in big oak casks. The proportions of the mixtures can vary, and taste can vary depending on the proportions. This vinegar is best to cook with.

Condiments

Certain condiments are highly popular in Italian cooking and we will take a look at the most popular ones in this section.

Chutney

These are flavor, usually quite spicy sauces of Indian origin. These are almost always made fresh using raw ingredients. Italian versions of chutneys usually contain vinegar too. These are easy to make and make for great sides with pretty much every main course.

Honey

Honey is another Italian staple that is enjoyed all over Italy. Honey is available in many flavors, depending on the flower the bees were made to collect from. Popular kinds of Italian honey are made from thyme, sage, acacia, lavender, and many more.

Mostarda

This is a condiment made using candied fruits and mustard syrup and has always been an important component of the Italian pantry.

Cheese

We Italians love our cheese. More than 460 kinds of cheese are produced in Italy! You don't need to know about all of them though. Below are some of the most popular varieties used in the recipes in this book. If you can't find these in a nearby store, you can always get them online on amazon.

- Asiago
- Bel paese
- Burrata
- Caciocavallo
- Caprino
- Castelmagno
- Fontina
- Gorgonzola
- Grana padano
- Mascarpone
- Montasio
- Mozzarella
- Parmigiano-reggiano
- Pecorino
- Provolone
- Ricotta
- Scamorza
- Taleggio

Pasta

Pasta is probably the second thing that comes to mind when someone mentions Italian food, the first probably being Pizza. You can buy pasta either fresh or dried. Fresh pasta is moist and tender, made using a wide variety of flours and other ingredients. Dried pasta is usually made using durum-wheat flour and water and then dried completely. Both kinds of pasta come in all shapes and sizes and are used in more kinds of recipes I can think of.

BREAKFAST

ZUCCHINI HAM ITALIAN QUICHE

PREPARATION
15 min

COOKING
50 min

SERVES
3

INGREDIENTS

- ½ cup of whole purpose flour
- 1 cup of grated cheddar cheese
- 3 green onions
- 1 ½ cups of milk
- 1 medium-sized zucchini, coarsely chopped
- 3 eggs
- 3 slices of ham, coarsely chopped
- 2 tablespoons of finely chopped parsley leaves

DIRECTIONS

1. In a bowl, whisk the milk, eggs, and flour until smooth and stir in the rest of the ingredients.
2. Bake the mixture for about 45 minutes at a temperature of 350 F.
3. Sprinkle the parsley and serve.

ITALIAN EGG TOAST

PREPARATION
5 min

COOKING
5 min

SERVES
3

INGREDIENTS

- ½ cup of pizza sauce
- 2 slices of bread
- 2 eggs
- 1 ½ tablespoons of olive oil
- 4 tablespoons of shredded mozzarella cheese
- Some Italian seasonings

DIRECTIONS

1. Heat the pizza sauce in a skillet and set aside.
2. Heat the oil in a skillet, crack in the eggs and cook until the whites are set.
3. Toast the bread slices, divide the pizza sauce, cheese, and eggs on each toast.

ITALIAN POACHED EGGS

PREPARATION
5 min

COOKING
7 min

SERVES
3

INGREDIENTS

- 2 tablespoons of olive oil
- 14 oz of tomatoes with herbs, diced
- ¼ teaspoon of minced garlic cloves
- 1 tablespoon of freshly chopped rosemary
- A dash of red pepper flakes
- 1 tablespoon of freshly chopped parsley
- 2 tablespoons of grated parmesan cheese
- 4 eggs

DIRECTIONS

1. Heat the oil in a skillet, add the parsley, tomatoes, garlic, and rosemary and bring to a boil.
2. Simmer for about 5-6 minutes and stir in the pepper flakes.
3. Make four hollows and crack an egg in each space.
4. Cover and cook until they are done.
5. Scoop the eggs with sauce on a plate and garnish with cheese and parsley.

BREAKFAST PEPPERONI PIZZA

PREPARATION
30 min

COOKING
55 min

SERVES
3

INGREDIENTS

- 2 eggs
- 1 green onion, chopped
- 2 teaspoons water
- 12 slices pepperoni

DIRECTIONS

1. Beat water, onion, and eggs, in a small bowl.
2. Heat butter in a small skillet until hot; pour in the egg mixture.
3. On medium heat, cook and stir until the eggs are partially set.
4. On an ungreased baking sheet, put the crust then top with 2 tbsp. of cheese; drizzle with approximately 2 tbsp. pizza sauce.
5. Add the scrambled egg mixture on top.
6. Drizzle the rest of the pizza sauce then scatter with the rest of the cheese.
7. Add pepperoni on top.
8. Bake for 10-12 mins in a 400 degrees F oven or until the crust is slightly crisp.
9. Let it sit for 5 mins and Serve.

VANILLA LACED TIRAMISU CREPES

PREPARATION
60 min

COOKING
5 min

SERVES
3

INGREDIENTS

- 4 eggs
- 2 tablespoons of brewed coffee
- ¼ cup of club soda
- ¾ cup of milk
- 3 tablespoons of melted butter
- 1 tablespoon of vanilla extract
- 1 cup of all-purpose flour
- ¼ teaspoon of salt
- 2 tablespoons of baking cocoa
- 3 tablespoons of sugar

FILLING

- 2 tablespoons of vanilla extract
- 8 oz of mascarpone cheese
- 1 cup of sugar
- ¼ cup of brewed coffee
- 8 oz of softened cream cheese
- Some whipped cream and cocoa

DIRECTIONS

1. In a bowl, whisk the milk, butter, eggs, coffee, vanilla, baking soda, and salt.
2. Cover and keep refrigerated for 55-65 minutes.
3. Heat a nonstick skillet over a medium heat and add two tablespoons of batter in, tilt to coat the pan evenly, and cook both sides for about 30 seconds.
4. Repeat the process with the remaining batter.
5. Cool and stack the crepes with paper towels in-between.

MAKE THE FILLING

1. Add the cheese and sugar into a bowl, beat until fluffy, and stir the vanilla extract in.
2. Place 2 tablespoons of the mixture on each crepe and roll them up.
3. Top with whipped cream and cocoa.

BRUNCH BAKE

PREPARATION
30 min

COOKING
55 min

SERVES
3

INGREDIENTS

- 12 eggs
- 1 pound of Italian sausage
- 1 onion, chopped
- 4 cups of shredded Italian cheese
- 1 pound of Portobello mushrooms, quartered
- 1 medium-sized green capsicum, chopped
- 1 medium-sized red capsicum, chopped
- 2 garlic cloves, minced
- 12 oz of baby spinach
- 8 slices of Italian bread, 1-inch thick
- 1 cup of milk
- ½ teaspoon of salt
- ½ teaspoon of pepper
- 1 teaspoon of Italian seasoning
- ¼ teaspoon of ground nutmeg

DIRECTIONS

1. Heat a skillet over medium heat; add the sausage, peppers, onion, mushrooms, and garlic. Cook until the pink color disappears.
2. Drain the excess liquid and set aside.
3. Sauté the spinach in a large, oiled skillet only until it wilts.
4. Place them into a baking sheet.
5. Broil for about 3 minutes until lightly brown and transfer into a baking dish.
6. Into a bowl, whisk the eggs, nutmeg, Italian seasoning, salt, and pepper.
7. Add a layer of the sausage mixture and spinach over the bread slices, top with the egg mixture, sprinkle with cheese, cover, and refrigerate overnight.
8. Allow to rest for 30 minutes after removing from the fridge.
9. Bake for about 60 minutes in a preheated oven at a temperature of 350 F and let it cool before serving.

BREAKFAST PIZZA SKILLET

PREPARATION
30 min

COOKING
45 min

SERVES
3

INGREDIENTS

- 1-pound Johnsonville® Ground Mild Italian sausage
- 5 cups frozen shredded hash brown potatoes
- 1/2 cup chopped onions
- 1/2 cup chopped green pepper
- 1/4 to 1/2 teaspoon salt
- Pepper to taste
- 1/2 cup sliced mushrooms
- 4 large eggs, lightly beaten
- 1 medium tomato, thinly sliced
- 1 cup shredded cheddar cheese
- Sour cream and salsa, optional

DIRECTIONS

1. Cook the sausage over medium heat in a large skillet until no longer pink.
2. Add pepper, salt, green pepper, onion, and potatoes.
3. Cook for 18-20 minutes over medium-high heat or until the potatoes become brown.
4. Stir in mushrooms.
5. Top the potato mixture with eggs.
6. Arrange sliced tomatoes on top.
7. Top with cheese.
8. Cook covered over medium-low heat until eggs become completely set [do not stir], or for 10-15 minutes.
9. Serve with salsa and sour cream if preferred.

BRUNCH RISOTTO

PREPARATION
30 min

COOKING
25 min

SERVINGS
3

INGREDIENTS

- 5 ¼ to 5 ¾ cups reduced-sodium chicken broth
- ¾-pound Italian turkey sausage links, casings removed
- 2 cups uncooked arborio rice
- 1 garlic clove, minced
- ¼ teaspoon pepper
- 1 tablespoon olive oil
- 1 medium tomato, chopped

DIRECTIONS

1. Heat broth in a big saucepan and keep warm.
2. Cook sausage in a big nonstick skillet until it isn't pink anymore, then drain and set aside.
3. Sauté pepper, garlic, and rice with oil in the same skillet about 2 to 3 minutes.
4. Turn the sausage back to the skillet.
5. Stir in 1 cup heated broth carefully, then cook and stir until the entire liquid is absorbed.
6. Put in 1/2 cup leftover broth at a time while stirring immediately.
7. Let the liquid absorb between additions.
8. Cook just until rice is nearly softened and risotto is creamy.
9. Cook for about 20 minutes in total.
10. Put in tomato and heat through, then serve promptly.

CALICO PEPPER FRITTATA

PREPARATION
30 min

COOKING
35 min

SERVINGS
3

INGREDIENTS

- 5 large eggs
- 1-1/4 cups egg substitute
- 1 tablespoon grated Romano cheese
- 1/2 teaspoon salt
- 1/8 teaspoon pepper
- 1 tablespoon olive oil
- 1 medium sweet red pepper, chopped
- 1 medium green pepper, chopped
- 1 jalapeno pepper, seeded and chopped
- 1 medium onion, chopped
- 1 garlic clove, minced

DIRECTIONS

1. Beat the first 5 ingredients in a big bowl until combined.
2. On medium-high heat, heat oil in a big nonstick pan.
3. Cook and stir onion and peppers in hot oil until tender.
4. Put in garlic then cook for another minute.
5. Add the egg mixture, it should set at the edges right away.
6. Cook for 8-10mins without cover until the eggs are set completely.
7. Push the cooked part to the middle and let the uncooked eggs flow beneath.
8. Slice into wedges.

CARAMELIZED MUSHROOM AND ONION FRITTATA

PREPARATION
30 min

COOKING
55 min

SERVES
3

INGREDIENTS

- 1-pound sliced fresh mushrooms
- 1 medium red onion, chopped
- 3 tablespoons butter
- 3 tablespoons olive oil
- 1 shallot, chopped
- 1 garlic clove, minced
- ½ cup shredded cheddar cheese
- ¼ cup shredded Parmesan cheese
- 8 large eggs
- 3 tablespoons heavy whipping cream
- ¼ teaspoon salt
- ¼ teaspoon pepper

DIRECTIONS

1. Add the butter and oil in a 10-in. ovenproof skillet, cook and stir the mushrooms and onion in until tender.
2. Adjust the heat to medium-low; allow them to cook for about half an hour or until it turns deep golden brown.
3. Stir the mixture from time to time.
4. Stir in the garlic and shallot; let it cook for 1 minute more.
5. Lower the heat; top it off with cheeses.
6. Whisk the cream, eggs, pepper, and salt in a big bowl; pour over top.
7. Allow to cook for 4-6 minutes while covered or until eggs are almost set.
8. Take off the cover of the skillet.
9. Broil, positioning the pan 3-4 in. away from the heat source for 2-3 minutes or until eggs are entirely set.
10. Let it rest for about 5 minutes.
11. Slice into wedges.

PASTA

COURGETTI LASAGNA

PREPARATION
10 min

COOKING
20 min

SERVINGS
2

INGREDIENTS

- 9 dried lasagna sheets
- 1 tablespoon of oil
- 1 onion, finely chopped
- 2 garlic cloves, minced
- 6 zucchinis, coarsely grated
- 8-oz (250g) tub of ricotta
- ½ cup of cheddar cheese
- 12 oz of tomato sauce

DIRECTIONS

1. Cook the lasagna sheets in boiling water until soft.
2. Rinse in cold water and drizzle with oil.
3. Sauté the onion, add the garlic and zucchini and cook until soft. Stir 2/3 of cheddar and ricotta in, then season.
4. Heat the tomato sauce until hot.
5. Layer the lasagna in a baking dish and add half of the zucchini mixture, pasta, and tomato sauce.
6. Repeat for another layer, top with blobs of ricotta, and sprinkle the cheese.
7. Bake until the pasta is tender, and the cheddar is golden.

VEGETARIAN CAPONATA PASTA

PREPARATION
5 min

COOKING
20 min

SERVINGS
2

INGREDIENTS

- 4 tablespoons of olive oil
- 1 large onion, finely chopped
- 4 garlic cloves, minced
- 12 oz of rigatoni or penne
- 1 tablespoon of small capers
- 14-oz can of diced tomatoes
- 8 oz [250g] of char-grilled Mediterranean veg, roughly chopped
- 2 tablespoons of raisins
- Some parmesan
- A bunch of basil leaves

DIRECTIONS

1. Fry the onions until tender, add the garlic and cook for 1 minute.
2. Add in the raisins, tomatoes, mixed vegetables, and capers.
3. Season and simmer until the sauce thickens.
4. Cook the pasta and drain, mix it with the sauce, sprinkle with basil leaves and parmesan.

SPAGHETTI WITH MEATBALLS

PREPARATION
30 min

COOKING
55 min

SERVINGS
3

INGREDIENTS

Meatballs
- 1-pound ground pork sausage
- 1-pound ground beef
- 2 cloves crushed garlic
- 2 tbsp. fresh basil, chopped
- ¾ cup grated parmesan
- 2 tbsp. fresh chives, chopped
- ½ tsp. black pepper powder
- ½ tsp. pepper flakes
- ¼ cup milk
- 1 tsp. salt
- 2 eggs
- ½ packet crackers, finely crushed

- Raw Marinara Sauce
- 1 can diced tomatoes
- ¼ cup fresh basil leaves
- 1 sprig fresh oregano leaves
- 1 garlic clove
- 5 oil-packed sun-dried tomato halves
- 1 tbsp. lemon juice
- 2 tbsp. olive oil
- ¼ tsp. salt
- Pinch of pepper

Pasta
- 1-pound spaghetti

DIRECTIONS

Meatballs:

1. Preheat oven to 400 degrees.
2. Combine all meatball ingredients in a large ball and mix by hand until just combined.
3. Divide and roll into golf-sized balls.
4. Place on a greased, foil-lined baking sheet.
5. Bake the meatballs for 20 minutes.

Sauce:

1. Combine all sauce ingredients in a blender and blend till smooth.
2. Pour into a large saucepan and bring to a simmer.
3. Carefully add in the meatballs and continue to simmer for an extra 10 minutes. Stir gently.

Pasta:

1. In a large pot, bring 4 quarts of water to a boil.
2. Sprinkle in salt.
3. Add the spaghetti and cook until done – 8 to 10 minutes.

To serve:

1. Layer spaghetti in a serving dish and top with meatball mixture.
2. Sprinkle with Parmesan cheese and enjoy!

MEXICAN MAC AND CHEESE

PREPARATION
30 min

COOKING
40 min

SERVES
3

INGREDIENTS

- Salt
- 8 ounces uncooked wagon wheel macaroni
- 2 tablespoons unsalted butter
- ½ tablespoon minced garlic
- 2 tablespoons all-purpose flour
- 1 teaspoon ground cumin
- ¾ cup finely chopped onion
- 2 cups milk
- 1 chipotle en adobo, chopped
- ½ teaspoon ground coriander
- ½ cup sundried tomatoes, thinly sliced
- 2 ¼ cups grated sharp Cheddar cheese
- 1 cup grated Jack cheese
- 1 ½ cups crushed tortilla chips
- 1 1/3 cups freshly grated Cotija cheese

DIRECTIONS

1. Cook the pasta according to package directions.
2. Remove, drain, and set aside.
3. Heat a 10-inch cast-iron skillet over med. heat until hot.
4. Add the butter, onion, garlic, cumin, and coriander, and cook over medium-low heat, stirring often, until the onion is softened, about 7 minutes.
5. Preheat your oven to 350°F.
6. Add the flour to the softened onions and stir continuously for 3 minutes.
7. Whisk in the milk and bring to a boil.
8. Reduce & simmer for 2 minutes.
9. Add the chipotle and tomatoes and cool slightly.
10. Add the cheeses and stir until melted.
11. Stir the pasta into the cheese mixture.
12. In a bowl, toss the tortilla chips and Cotija cheese together and drizzle on top of the macaroni.
13. Bake until the dish is hot, and the top is golden brown, 25 to 30 minutes.
14. Serve.

PASTA PIZZA CHICKEN CASSEROLE

PREPARATION
30 min

COOKING
40 min

SERVES
3

INGREDIENTS

- 4 cups cooked small shell pasta
- 2 cups shredded cooked chicken
- 1 jar (16 ounces) pizza sauce
- 1 small onion, sliced
- ½ green bell pepper, sliced

DIRECTIONS

1. Preheat oven to 350 degrees.
2. Mix all the ingredients in a greased 9x13-inch casserole dish.
3. Cover and bake for 25 mins. or until heated through.
4. Serve.

ARRABIATA SAUCE

PREPARATION
10 min

COOKING
20 min

SERVINGS
3

INGREDIENTS

- 1 tsp. olive oil
- 1 cup onion, finely chopped
- 4 cloves garlic, minced
- 7 tbsp. red wine
- 1 tbsp. white sugar
- 1 tbsp. fresh basil, roughly chopped
- ½ tsp. Italian seasoning
- ¼ tsp. black pepper
- 2 14.5-ounce cans of tomatoes, peeled and finely diced
- 2 tbsp. of parsley, roughly chopped

DIRECTIONS

1. First heat up the oil.
2. Once the oil is hot enough add in the garlic and onions and cook for at least five minutes.
3. Then add in the wine, white sugar, fresh basil, peppers, tomato paste, fresh lemon juice, Italian seasoning, tomatoes, and a dash of pepper.
4. Stir thoroughly to combine and bring to a boil.
5. Reduce the heat to low and allow to simmer for the next 15 minutes.
6. After this time add in the fresh parsley and remove from heat.
7. Serve over a bed of pasta and enjoy.

LASAGNA

PREPARATION
10 min

COOKING
20 min

SERVINGS
3

INGREDIENTS

- Unsalted butter, for the dish
- 1 recipe (4 cups) Thick Béchamel
- ½ recipe (6 sheets; about 8 ounces) Fresh Pasta Sheet
- ½ recipe (3 cups) Ragu Bolognese, warm
- 4 oz. freshly grated Parmesan cheese

DIRECTIONS

Preheat oven to 375F.

Assemble the lasagna:

1. Mix together ½ cup of the béchamel sauce and ¼ cup of room-temperature water and put in a 9 by 13inch (3-quart) glass or ceramic baking dish, then top with one-third of the noodles (2 sheets).
2. Put 1 cup of the béchamel sauce on the pasta and cover with 1½ cups of the Bolognese sauce.
3. Sprinkle with ⅓ cup of the Parmesan.
4. Repeat with another layer of noodles, 1 cup of the béchamel, the remaining Bolognese sauce, and ⅓ cup of the Parmesan. Top with the remaining noodles, béchamel, and Parmesan.

Bake the lasagna:

1. Cover with foil and bake for 30 mins. Uncover & bake until bubbling and the top is golden, about 20 minutes longer.
2. Let rest for 15 minutes before cutting into squares and serving.

SPICY PASTA ALFREDO CASSEROLE

PREPARATION
10 min

COOKING
30 min

SERVINGS
3

INGREDIENTS

- 1 [12 oz.] package fettuccini
- ½ cup butter
- 2 cups heavy cream
- ½ cup water
- 2 clove garlic, crushed
- 3 cups grated Parmesan cheese
- ½ cup fresh parsley, chopped
- 1 [16 oz.] carton sour cream
- 1 can diced tomatoes & green chiles, drained
- 1 [14 oz.] jar artichoke hearts, drained, quartered
- 1 jar roasted red peppers, first drained, & chopped

DIRECTIONS

1. Cook fettuccini according to package instructions; drain well and set aside.
2. In a med saucepan, melt the butter on med heat.
3. Stir in heavy cream and water; simmer for 5 minutes. Mix in garlic and 2 cups cheese.
4. Whisk quickly, heating through.
5. Remove from heat and stir in parsley.
6. Stir in sour cream and tomatoes with green chiles.
7. Combine pasta, sauce, artichoke hearts, and red peppers.
8. Spoon into a greased 9x13x2-inch baking dish.
9. Cover & bake at 350F. for 45 minutes.
10. Add the last cup of cheese on top.
11. Bake for 10 minutes more.

TORTELLINI CHICKEN PRIMAVERA

PREPARATION
10 min

COOKING
20 min

SERVINGS
3

INGREDIENTS

- 1 1/2 to 2 lbs. boneless, skinless chicken breast meat, cubed
- 2 to 3 cloves garlic, minced
- ½ tablespoon dried basil
- 1 ½ cups water
- 3 cups tortellini
- 1 container pesto sauce
- 3 to 4 Roma tomatoes, chopped
- 1 red bell pepper, chopped
- 1 yellow bell pepper, chopped
- 1 zucchini, sliced
- Parmesan cheese, shredded, for garnish

DIRECTIONS

1. In a Dutch oven, stew chicken, garlic, and basil with water.
2. Cook over med-high heat till all the water evaporates.
3. In a separate pan, cook pasta as directed on package until al dente; drain.
4. In a large serving dish, toss pasta, chicken, and pesto sauce with bell peppers and zucchini.
5. Sprinkle with Parmesan cheese.
6. Serve.

ITALIAN MACARONI AND CHEESE

PREPARATION
10 min

COOKING
40 min

SERVINGS
3

INGREDIENTS

- 12 oz of short spiral pasta
- 8 oz (250g) of grated vegetarian cheddar
- ½ cup of baguette, chopped into small chunks
- 3 tablespoons of butter
- 1 teaspoon of mustard powder
- 3 tablespoons of flour
- 2 cups (500ml) of milk
- ¼ cup of grated parmesan

DIRECTIONS

1. Spread the baguette on a baking sheet and drizzle with 1 tablespoon of melted butter.
2. Season and bake until crispy.
3. Cook the pasta, drain and set aside.
4. Melt the butter.
5. Cook the garlic and mustard, stir the flour and milk in, cook for 1 minute, and simmer until it thickens.
6. Take it off of the heat, add cheddar and parmesan and stir the pasta in.
7. Season, sprinkle with parmesan, and bake until golden.

GREEN TOMATO PASTA

PREPARATION
10 min

COOKING
40 min

SERVES
3

INGREDIENTS

- 4 cups spaghetti
- 4 large green tomatoes, thinly sliced [1/8-inch thick]
- Salt and pepper, to taste
- 1 cup flour
- Vegetable oil, for frying
- 2 garlic cloves, minced
- ¼ cup parmesan cheese, grated

DIRECTIONS

1. Prepare spaghetti according to directions; & drain well and set aside.
2. Season tomatoes with salt and pepper.
3. Coat with flour & fry in hot oil with garlic until golden brown.
4. Do not overcook. Place fried tomato slices on top of hot, cooked pasta.
5. Top with parmesan cheese and serve immediately.

PILLI PILLI PASTA SAUCE

PREPARATION
10 min

COOKING
20 min

SERVES
3

INGREDIENTS

- Tomato Sauce [2 cups]
- Lemon Juice [½ cup]
- Onions [½ cup, minced]
- Garlic Powder [1 tbsp.]
- Red Crushed Pepper [1 tbsp.]

DIRECTIONS

1. Put all ingredients into a two-quart bowl and blend to combine.
2. Cover the container and refrigerate.
3. Enjoy with seafood or use as a relish.

PASTA MILANO

PREPARATION
10 min

COOKING
20 min

SERVES
3

INGREDIENTS

- 1-pound bowtie pasta
- 2 tsp olive oil
- 1-pound chicken, chopped into small piece
- 1 12-ounce package mushrooms, chopped
- 1 cup onion, minced
- 2 garlic cloves, finely minced
- ½ cup sun-dried tomatoes, diced
- 1½ cups half and half
- 1 tbsp. butter, softened
- ½ cup Parmesan cheese, shredded, plus some more for serving
- 1 tsp black pepper, ground
- 1 tbsp. fresh basil, minced

DIRECTIONS

1. Follow instructions on the package to cook bowtie pasta.
2. Drain, then set aside.
3. Add oil to a pan over med-high heat.
4. Once hot, add chicken and stir-fry for about 5 to 6 minutes until cooked through.
5. Set chicken aside onto a plate.
6. In the same pan, toss in mushrooms, onions, garlic, and sundried tomatoes.
7. Sauté until onions turn soft and mushrooms become a light brown, then sprinkle salt and pepper to season.
8. Return chicken to pan and mix.
9. Mix half and half, butter, Parmesan, pepper, and basil in a small bowl.
10. Add half and half mixture to pan.
11. Stir, and let simmer for about 3 to 4 minutes or until pan ingredients are thoroughly heated.
12. Mix in pasta until coated well.
13. Serve

LEMON CHICKEN WITH PASTA

PREPARATION
10 min

COOKING
30 min

SERVES
3

INGREDIENTS

- Chicken breast (1 lb./454 g)
- Large lemon (1)
- Shirataki angel hair noodles (2, 7-oz./200 g pkg.)
- Garlic (1 large clove)
- XCT oil/another cooking oil (1 tbsp.)
- Organic garlic (1 large clove)
- Dried oregano (.5 tsp.) or Minced fresh oregano - leaves only (1 tsp.)
- Himalayan pink salt (.5 tsp.)
- Butter or ghee (2 tbsp.)
- Collagelatin/another grass-fed gelatin (1 tbsp.)
- Fresh oregano - leaves only (1-2 tbsp.)

DIRECTIONS

1. Squeeze the juice and zest from the lemon into separate containers.
2. Prepare the noodles, and rinse for 15 seconds.
3. Boil for two minutes in a saucepan of boiling water.
4. Drain the noodles and arrange them in a dry skillet using the medium temperature heat setting.
5. "Dry roast" them for one minute.
6. Cool them in the pan for two to three minutes.
7. Using the med-high temperature setting, warm a cast-iron skillet with oil.
8. Mince the chicken into small pieces and toss into the skillet with the minced garlic, salt, and dried oregano.
9. Sauté until thoroughly cooked for about eight to ten minutes.
10. Stir occasionally.
11. Transfer the chicken into a mixing bowl and set it aside.
12. Lower the pan temperature setting to medium.
13. Pour in the lemon juice to deglaze the pan. Add butter and whisk in the gelatin to finish.
14. Mix the noodles and chicken back into the skillet, tossing thoroughly to combine.
15. Serve topped with lemon zest and a garnish of fresh oregano.

MUSHROOM BACON PASTA

PREPARATION
5 min

COOKING
20 min

SERVINGS
3

INGREDIENTS

- 14 oz of penne pasta
- 8-oz (250g) package of button mushrooms, sliced
- 4 tablespoons of pesto
- 8 rashers of streaky bacon, cut into small pieces
- A handful of basil leaves
- ¾ cup (180ml) of crème Fraiche

DIRECTIONS

1. Cook the pasta in salted boiling water, drain and set aside.
2. Fry the bacon and mushrooms until golden.
3. Add the pasta and some water in and cook stirring for 2 minutes.
4. Take it off of the heat and spoon the pesto and crème Fraiche in.
5. Add basil and stir.
6. Sprinkle with basil and serve.

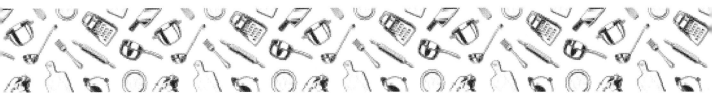

SPICY SPAGHETTI WITH MUSHROOMS

PREPARATION
10 min

COOKING
15 min

SERVINGS
4

INGREDIENTS

- 12-oz of spaghetti
- 8-oz (250g) package of chestnut mushrooms, thinly sliced
- 1 garlic clove, minced
- 1 onion, finely chopped
- 14-oz can of diced tomatoes
- ½ deseeded red chili, finely chopped
- 2 tablespoons of olive oil
- 1 celery, finely chopped
- A bunch of parsley

DIRECTIONS

1. Fry the mushrooms with 1 tablespoon of oil until soft and golden.
2. Fry the garlic in, add some parsley, and set aside.
3. Fry the onion and celery until slightly brown, stir the tomatoes, salt, and chili in, bring to a boil and simmer until it thickens.
4. Boil the spaghetti according to the instructions on the package and drain.
5. Toss with the sauce and top with the mushrooms.

ITALIAN LINGUINE WITH AVOCADO

PREPARATION
20 min

COOKING
10 min

SERVES
2

INGREDIENTS

- 8 oz (230g) of wholemeal linguine
- 2 medium-sized avocados, chopped
- 4 ripe tomatoes, chopped
- 1 red chili, deseeded and chopped
- Juice and zest of 1 ½ lime
- 1 pack of chopped fresh coriander
- 2 small red onions, finely chopped

DIRECTIONS

1. Cook the pasta in boiling water until soft.
2. Into a bowl, mix the avocado, zest, lime juice, tomatoes, onion, chili, and coriander.
3. Drain the pasta, toss it with the avocado mixture and serve.

APPETIZERS

ITALIAN HOAGIE DIP

PREPARATION
20 min

COOKING
40 min

SERVINGS
3

INGREDIENTS

- 8 slices of provolone cheese, diced
- 1 tablespoon of Italian seasoning
- 3 cups of romaine lettuce, finely chopped
- ¼ pound of diced deli ham
- ¼ pound of Genoa salami
- ¼ pound of diced pepperoni
- ½ cup of diced onions
- ½ cup of mayonnaise

DIRECTIONS

1. In a bowl, combine the meats, onions, and cheese.
2. Stir the mayonnaise and Italian seasoning in.
3. Stir in the lettuce and serve with crackers.

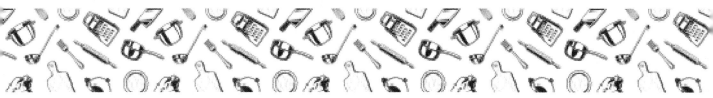

ASPARAGUS SALAD

PREPARATION
10 min

COOKING
0 min

SERVINGS
4

INGREDIENTS

- 1-pound asparagus, trimmed
- ½ cup water
- 5 tablespoons olive oil
- 8 slices of prosciutto, chopped
- 2 oranges, peeled, cut into segments
- 1 tablespoon orange juice
- ½ cup pistachios, roasted and chopped
- Salt and black pepper to the taste
- 1-ounce parmesan cheese, grated

DIRECTIONS

1. Put asparagus in a heatproof dish, add the water, salt, pepper, and 1 tablespoon olive oil, toss to coat, introduce in your microwave and cook on High for 5 minutes.
2. Divide asparagus on serving plates; add prosciutto and oranges on top.
3. Divide pistachios, the rest of the oil, and the orange juice on each serving plate.
4. Season with more salt and pepper if needed, sprinkle parmesan at the end and serve.

QUINCE SALAD

PREPARATION
10 min

COOKING
45 min

SERVINGS
4

INGREDIENTS

- 2 tablespoons olive oil
- Salt and black pepper to the taste
- 4 ounces prosciutto, cut into strips
- 2 tablespoons honey
- 2 lemon zest strips
- 1-pound quinces, peeled, cored, and cut into quarters
- 4 cups baby arugula
- 2 ounces manchego, shaved
- 4 teaspoons balsamic vinegar
- 1/3 cup almonds, toasted and chopped

DIRECTIONS

1. Put quinces in a pot.
2. Add lemon zest, honey, and some water to cover them, bring to a boil over medium-high heat, cover, simmer for 45 minutes, take off heat and leave aside to cool down.
3. In a salad bowl, mix arugula with ham, oil, salt, and pepper.
4. Slice quince quarters and add to salad bowl.
5. Add almonds, and manchego, drizzle balsamic vinegar all over and serve.

NOT USUAL POTATO SALAD

PREPARATION
10 min

COOKING
20 min

SERVINGS
8

INGREDIENTS

- 2 teaspoons marjoram, chopped
- For the salad:
- ¼ cup rice vinegar
- 1 tablespoon olive oil
- 3 and ¼ pounds baby red potatoes
- 2 cup frozen artichoke hearts
- ¼ cup lemon juice
- Salt and black pepper to the taste
- 2 teaspoons Dijon mustard
- ¼ cup olive oil
- 2 garlic cloves, minced and mashed
- ½ teaspoon red pepper flakes
- Salt and black pepper to the taste
- ¾ cup mint, chopped
- 1 cup black olives, pitted and chopped

DIRECTIONS

1. In a bowl, mix lemon juice with salt, pepper, mustard, ¼ cup oil, 2 garlic cloves, marjoram, and pepper flakes and whisk well.

2. In a bowl, mix vinegar with salt and whisk well.

3. Put potatoes in a pot, add salt and water to cover, bring to a boil over high heat, reduce temperature, cook for 10 minutes, take off heat, drain, cool them down, peel, and cut them into chunks.

4. Put potatoes in a salad bowl, add rice vinegar mixed with salt and toss to coat.

5. Heat up a pan with 1 tablespoon oil over medium-high heat, add artichoke hearts and some salt and brown on both sides.

6. Add these over potatoes, also add mint and olives.

7. Add salt and pepper to the taste and the vinaigrette you've made at the beginning, toss to coat, and serve.

TORTELLINI SALAD

PREPARATION
10 min

COOKING
25 min

SERVINGS
4

INGREDIENTS

- 1 package tri-colored cheese tortellini
- ½ cup diced pepperoni
- ¼ cup sliced scallions
- 1 diced green bell pepper
- 1 cup halved cherry tomatoes
- ¾ cup chopped marinated artichoke hearts
- 6 oz. diced mozzarella cheese
- 1/3 cup Italian dressing

DIRECTIONS

1. Prepare the tortellini according to directions and drain.
2. Combine the tortellini with the remaining ingredients except the dressing and toss well.
3. Drizzle with the dressing.
4. Chill for 2 hours.

CAPRESE PASTA SALAD

PREPARATION
10 min

COOKING
35 min

SERVINGS
4

INGREDIENTS

- 2 cups cooked penne pasta
- 1 cup pesto
- 2 chopped tomatoes
- 1 cup diced mozzarella cheese
- Salt and pepper to taste
- 1/8 tsp. oregano
- 2 tsp. red wine vinegar

DIRECTIONS

1. Prepare the pasta according to directions, about 12 minutes. Drain.
2. Toss the pasta, pesto, tomatoes, cheese, and season with salt, pepper, and oregano.
3. Drizzle with red wine vinegar.
4. Refrigerate for 1 hour.

FRIED CALAMARI

PREPARATION
10 min

COOKING
15 min

SERVINGS
6

INGREDIENTS

- 2 lb. cleaned squid, cut into circles
- ¼ cup canola oil
- 1 cup flour
- Salt and pepper to taste
- ¼ tsp. crush red pepper or more to taste
- 3 minced garlic cloves

DIRECTIONS

1. Wash the squid thoroughly and salt and pepper the pieces.
2. Combine the flour and crushed red pepper in a paper bag with the squid.
3. Shake to coat and set aside.
4. Next, heat the oil in your skillet until it is very hot.
5. Sauté the garlic for 30 seconds.
6. Then, add the calamari and fry for 1 minute 30 seconds. Do not over-fry.
7. Serve with Sriracha sauce as a dip.
8. If children are enjoying this, stir some mayonnaise into the Sriracha to remove the heat.

KALAMATA CAVIAR

PREPARATION
10 min

COOKING
45 min

SERVES
4

INGREDIENTS

- 4 cloves garlic, peeled
- 2 tablespoons olive oil

DIRECTIONS

1. In a food processor, blend feta cheese, kalamata olives, pecans, olive oil, and garlic.
2. Adjust the amount of olive oil if necessary, to attain a pesto-like consistency.

KALAMATA OLIVE TAPENADE

PREPARATION
10 min

COOKING
25 min

SERVINGS
4

INGREDIENTS

- 3 cloves garlic, peeled
- 2 tablespoons capers
- 3 tablespoons chopped fresh parsley
- 2 tablespoons lemon juice
- 2 tablespoons olive oil
- salt and pepper to taste

DIRECTIONS

1. In a food processor or a blender, put the garlic cloves and pulse to mince.
2. Put in olive oil, lemon juice, parsley, capers, and olives.
3. Process until the mixture is evenly chopped.
4. Add pepper and salt to taste.

LISA'S ITALIAN NACHOS

PREPARATION
10 min

COOKING
35 min

SERVINGS
4

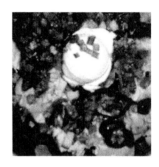

INGREDIENTS

- 2 pounds bulk Italian sausage
- 1-pound pepperoni, sliced
- 1 teaspoon crushed red pepper flakes
- 1 [28 ounce] jar spaghetti sauce
- 1 [8 ounce] jar salsa
- 1 [18 ounce] package tortilla chips
- 4 cups crumbled feta cheese
- 1 onion, chopped
- 1 cup sliced jalapeno peppers
- 2 cups black olives, drained and sliced
- 1 ½ cups sour cream

DIRECTIONS

1. Place a big frying pan on medium-high heat, and add crushed red pepper flakes, sliced pepperoni, and Italian sausage.
2. Stir and cook for 8 minutes until the sausage has cooked through and fully browned.
3. Strain the grease from the frying pan.
4. Mix in salsa and spaghetti sauce.
5. Cook for 5 minutes until the sauce and meat are hot.
6. On a very big dish, spread tortilla chips.
7. Evenly spoon over the chips with the hot meat sauce; and put sour cream, black olives, jalapenos, chopped onions, and feta cheese on top.

LASAGNA STUFFED MUSHROOMS

PREPARATION
10 min

COOKING
25 min

SERVES
4

INGREDIENTS

- ¼-pound lean ground beef
- ½ cup fat-free small curd cottage cheese
- 1 egg
- 1 tablespoon finely chopped green onion
- 1 tablespoon chopped fresh parsley
- Salt and black pepper to taste

DIRECTIONS

1. Set the oven to 375°F [190°C] and start preheating.
2. Coat an 8x8-inch baking dish using a cooking spray.
3. In a skillet, cook and stir the ground beef over medium heat, breaking it apart while cooking, about 10 minutes, until the meat is no longer pink. In a bowl, combine pepper, salt, parsley, green onion, egg, and cottage cheese until well combined.
4. Mix in the cooked ground beef.
5. In the prepared baking dish, place the mushrooms upside down, close together.
6. Spoon about 1 tablespoon cheese mixture into each mushroom's cavity and pour the remaining of the mixture into the dish to overflow between mushrooms.
7. Bake in the oven for about 15 minutes until the cheese filling is set.
8. Take the dish out of the oven, and evenly pour the pasta sauce over the mushrooms.
9. Drizzle an even layer of mozzarella cheese over the sauce, place the dish back into the oven, and broil for about 5 more minutes, until the cheese starts browning and bubbling.
10. Allow to rest for 5 minutes and serve.

BULGUR AND GRAPE SALAD

PREPARATION
10 min

COOKING
60 min

SERVINGS
6

INGREDIENTS

- ¼ cup parsley, chopped
- 1/3 cup walnuts, toasted and chopped
- 3 tablespoons walnut oil
- 3 tablespoons balsamic vinegar
- 1 cup red grapes, cut in quarters
- 1 cup bulgur
- 1 cup celery, chopped
- 3 tablespoons dried currants
- Salt and black pepper to the taste
- 2 tablespoons shallot, minced
- 1 cup water

DIRECTIONS

1. Put the water in a pot, bring to a boil over medium-high heat, add bulgur, take off heat and leave aside for 1 hour.
2. Fluff bulgur and transfer to a bowl.
3. Add celery, grapes, parsley, walnuts, walnut oil, currants, shallot, salt, pepper, and vinegar, toss to coat, and serve.

CHICKPEAS SALAD

PREPARATION
10 min

COOKING
90 min

SERVINGS
4

INGREDIENTS

- 3 potatoes
- 1 cup yogurt
- ¼ cup sour cream
- 1 tablespoon ginger, grated
- 1 teaspoon fennel seeds, toasted and ground
- 1and ½ teaspoons cumin, toasted and ground
- 1 cucumber, chopped
- 1 hot green chili pepper, chopped
- 1 red onion, chopped
- ¼ cup mint, chopped
- 3 cups canned chickpeas, drained
- 2 bay leaves
- ¼ teaspoon turmeric
- Salt and black pepper to the taste
- 1 yellow onion, cut in half
- ¼ cup cilantro, chopped
- 8 cups water

DIRECTIONS

1. Put beans in a pot, add the water over them, bring to a boil over medium-high heat, add bay leaves, yellow onion, salt, pepper, and turmeric, stir, reduce to medium and cook for 1 hour and 30 minutes, take off heat and leave aside to cool down.

2. Meanwhile, put potatoes in another pot, add salt, bring to a boil over high heat, cook for 20 minutes, drain, leave aside to cool down, peel and cut them into small cubes.

3. In a bowl, mix yogurt with sour cream, cumin, ginger, chili pepper, and fennel and whisk well.

4. In a bowl mix chickpea with red onion, potatoes, and cucumber.

5. Add mint, cilantro, more salt, and pepper to the taste and the yogurt dressing.

6. Toss to coat and serve after 15 minutes.

ITALIAN CREAMY DIP

PREPARATION
5 min

COOKING
45 min

SERVINGS
4

INGREDIENTS

- 1/8 teaspoon of onion powder 1 cup of sour cream
- ½ teaspoon of garlic salt
- ¼ teaspoon of Italian seasoning

DIRECTIONS

1. Mix all the ingredients in a bowl.
2. Refrigerate for about 70 minutes for the flavors to blend and serve.

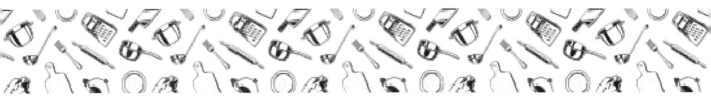

ROSEMARY BAKED OLIVES AND ORANGE

PREPARATION	COOKING	SERVINGS
25 min	**15** min	**12**

INGREDIENTS

- 2 ½ teaspoons of chopped oregano
- ¼ teaspoon of crushed red pepper flakes
- 3 ½ cups of whole mixed olives
- 2 tablespoons of orange juice
- ¼ cup of dry white wine
- 2 garlic cloves, minced
- 2 tablespoons of olive oil
- 2 sprigs of rosemary
- 2 tablespoons of chopped parsley
- 2 tablespoons of grated orange zest

DIRECTIONS

1. Preheat the oven to 375 F.
2. Add the wine, olives, olive oil, garlic, and orange juice in a baking dish and stir.
3. Nestle the rosemary in the olive mixture and bake in the oven for 14-17 minutes.
4. Stir after 8 minutes.
5. Remove the rosemary; stir the parsley, zest, pepper, and oregano in.
6. Serve while warm.

PIZZA

SAUSAGE & MUSHROOM PIZZA FRITTATA

PREPARATION
10 min

COOKING
45 min

SERVINGS
4

INGREDIENTS

- 4 oz Johnsonville® Ground Mild Italian sausage
- 2 cups sliced fresh mushrooms
- 2 tbsps. finely chopped red onion
- 2 tbsps. finely chopped green pepper
- ¼ cup finely chopped fresh pineapple
- 6 large eggs, beaten
- 6 tbsps. marinara sauce
- 2 tbsps. shredded part-skim mozzarella cheese
- 2 tbsps. grated Parmigiano-Reggiano cheese
- 2 tbsps. minced fresh parsley

DIRECTIONS

1. Preheat the broiler.
2. On medium heat, cook pepper, sausage, onion, and mushrooms for 6-8 mins while crumbling the sausage in a 10-inch ovenproof pan until the veggies are tender and sausage is not pink; drain.
3. Put the sausage mixture back in the pan then mix in pineapple.
4. Add beaten eggs; cook for 4-6 mins while covered until almost set.
5. Slather the marinara all over then top with cheeses.
6. Broil for 2-3 mins, three to four inches from heat until the cheese melts and eggs are set completely.
7. Let it sit for 5 mins.
8. Top with parsley then slice into wedges.

MARGHERITA PIZZA

PREPARATION
10 min

COOKING
25 min

SERVINGS
4

INGREDIENTS

- 10 fresh basil leaves, washed, dried
- 2 cloves garlic, minced
- ¼ cup olive oil
- Salt to taste
- 8 tomatoes, sliced
- 2 baked pizza crusts
- 8 oz. Mozzarella cheese, shredded
- 4 oz. Fontina cheese, shredded
- ½ cup Parmesan cheese, grated
- ½ cup crumbled feta cheese

DIRECTIONS

1. Combine the garlic, olive oil, and salt.
2. Toss the tomatoes in this mixture.
3. Marinate for 15 minutes.
4. Preheat your oven to 400 degrees F.
5. Brush the pizza crust with tomato marinade.
6. Sprinkle with the cheese.
7. Top with the tomato mixture.
8. Add the rest of the ingredients on top of the pizza.
9. Bake in the oven for 10 minutes.

SPINACH BRUNCH PIZZA

PREPARATION
10 min

COOKING
30 min

SERVINGS
4

INGREDIENTS

- 2/3 cup reduced-fat biscuit/baking mix
- 2 tbsps. plus 1 tsp. water
- 2 cups fresh baby spinach, chopped
- ½ cup egg substitute
- 1/3 cup sour cream
- 1/3 cup shredded reduced-fat cheddar cheese
- 2 green onions, chopped
- ½ tsp. garlic powder
- 2 bacon strips, cooked and crumbled

DIRECTIONS

1. Mix water and biscuit mix in a small bowl to make a soft dough.
2. Coat a 7 in. pie plate by cooking spray, press dough up the sides and onto the bottom.
3. Bake for 5 minutes at 450 degrees till becomes golden brown.
4. Get out of the oven.
5. Lower the heat to 375 degrees.
6. Mix garlic powder, onions, cheese, sour cream, egg substitute, spinach in a small bowl.
7. Transfer the mixture into the crust. Use bacon to sprinkle.
8. Bake till becomes golden brown, about 25 to 30 minutes.

PESTO PIZZA

PREPARATION
10 min

COOKING
30 min

SERVINGS
4

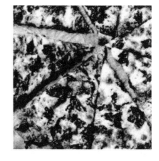

INGREDIENTS

- 1 pizza crust
- ½ cup pesto
- 1 onion, chopped
- 2 green bell peppers, chopped
- 2 oz. black olives, drained
- 1 tomato, sliced
- 4 oz. artichoke hearts, sliced
- 1 cup feta cheese, crumbled

DIRECTIONS

1. 1. Preheat your oven to 450 degrees F.
2. 2. Spread the pesto sauce on top of the pizza crust.
3. 3. Sprinkle the veggies and cheese on top.
4. 4. Bake in the oven for 10 minutes.

PIZZA CALZONE

PREPARATION
10 min

COOKING
30 min

SERVES
4

INGREDIENTS

Crust:
- 2 1/2 – 3 cups flour
- 1 [.25 oz.] package dry yeast
- 1/2 teaspoon salt
- 1 cup warm water [120 degrees F.]
- 2 tablespoons oil

Filling:
- 1 lb. ground meat, beef or pork
- 1 cup onion, chopped
- 1/2 cup green bell pepper, chopped
- 2 tomatoes, chopped
- 1/3 cup tomato paste
- 1 teaspoon basil
- 1/2 teaspoon thyme
- 1/2 teaspoon salt
- 3 tablespoons water
- 1 1/2 cups mozzarella cheese, shredded
- 1 egg, slightly beaten with 1 tablespoon water

DIRECTIONS

Crust

1. In a large bowl, combine 1 1/4 cups flour, yeast, and salt.
2. vAdd warm water and oil.
3. Beat at low speed in an electric mixer for 30 seconds, scraping sides of the bowl.
4. Beat 3 minutes on high.
5. Stir in remaining flour to form a dough; turn out on a floured board and knead 6 to 8 minutes.
6. Cover and let rest 10 minutes.
7. Divide into 6 parts and roll into 8-inch circles.
8. Let rise for 20 minutes.

Filling

1. Cook ground meat with onion and bell pepper until vegetables are tender.
2. Drain.
3. Combine tomatoes, tomato paste, basil, thyme, salt, and 3 tablespoons water.
4. Add to meat mixture.
5. Spoon onto crust circles.
6. Sprinkle with mozzarella cheese.
7. Moisten edge of dough with a mixture of egg and water.
8. Fold in half.
9. Seal edges.
10. Prick tops.
11. Brush with egg mixture.
12. Bake on a greased baking sheet and bake at 375 degrees F. for 25 to 30 minutes.

SWEET PIZZA DOUGH

PREPARATION
10 min

COOKING
20 min

SERVES
4

INGREDIENTS

- 1 cup all-purpose flour
- 1 cup 00 flour
- 1 teaspoon sugar
- ¼ teaspoon kosher salt
- ¾ cup very cold unsalted butter, cut into 12 equal cubes, divided
- ½ cup ice water

DIRECTIONS

1. In a bowl fitted with the paddle attachment of a stand mixer, mix together sugar, flour, and salt.
2. Add 8 of the butter cubes and mix on low speed until the butter begins to break down and the mixture has a sandy appearance.
3. Stop the mixer and sort through the unformed dough by hand, using your fingers to pinch together any large chunks of butter that remain.
4. Mix on low for 2 or 4 more turns.
5. Add the remaining 4 butter cubes and again mix on low until the butter is slightly incorporated about 2 minutes.
6. Stop the mixer and remove the work bowl.
7. Repeat the pinching step and make sure there are no remaining large chunks of butter in the mixture.
8. Make a well in the center of the shaggy mass.
9. Add the ice water to the well and gently cover the water pool with the surrounding dough crumbs.
10. Let the dough stand for 5 minutes to allow it to absorb some of the water.
11. Mix the dough by hand, quickly and evenly.
12. Knead the dough only long enough so it forms a moist, slightly sticky ball, being careful not to overwork it.
13. Divide the dough into two equal portions and wrap each in plastic wrap.
14. Flatten each ball into a smooth disc about ½ inch thick. The dough should have a nice, even marbled appearance, streaked with butter.
15. Refrigerate the dough until ready to use, at least 2 hours and up to 24 hours.

ROMAN-STYLE PIZZA

PREPARATION
15 min

COOKING
14 min

SERVES
3

INGREDIENTS

- 3.5g dried powdered yeast
- 650 ml water at room temperature
- 20g sea salt
- 1 kg wholewheat flour, unbleached and stoneground
- 25ml extra virgin olive oil
- ½ tsp sugar, superfine

DIRECTIONS

1. In a mixer, put the flour with a dough hook attachment.

2. In 100 ml of water, dissolve the yeast and add the flour with the 400 ml water that remained and the superfine sugar.

3. Turn on the mixer to the lowest setting and mix for 2 minutes until the water is absorbed totally. Add salt and water and mix together. Adding the water slowly little by little, double the mixer speed and add more water once the previous amount you put is absorbed. Don't worry if the mixture looks quite wet, just keep mixing for 8-10 minutes and the dough will gradually start stretching and it will form long gluten strands.

4. In a mixer bowl, rest the dough for 10 minutes while it's covered with a plastic wrap before you fold it. Leave it in the refrigerator to mature and form into three sheets of roman style pizza dough.

5. Shaping your Roman-style dough:

6. When the dough has rested briefly, to give it strength, it needs to be folded. Use a teaspoon of extra virgin olive oil to oil your hands and also oil the work surface lightly. Remove the dough from the container to a work surface. To form pockets of air, gently lift in the center and fold the ends under and meet in the middle.

7. Repeat the fold and turn the dough at 90 degrees. Cover the bowl with a plastic wrap and let it rest for 15 minutes and again fold. Leave to rest for another 15 minutes and do a final folding as before. Get a plastic container with an airtight lid and oil it and put the dough in there. Put in the refrigerator and leave for 18-24 hours.

8. When the dough matures once in the refrigerator, remove from the container and put on a work surface and divide the dough into 3 pieces.

9. To form a ball, shape each piece of dough by putting your hands under the outer edges and slide. Repeat this several times until the dough gets a ball-like appearance.

10. Using your fingers, gather and fold at the edge of every piece of dough and bring the balls towards you. This makes the ball smooth and even. Dough balls should be left to rise again for 2 hours at room temperature in three oiled contained containers.

11. Oil with extra virgin olive oil a baking tray or oven tray, on a work surface, put flour and turn one piece of dough. On the dough surface, start pressing gently using your fingers to roughly fit the tray size by stretching it.

12. Without a fan, preheat the oven to 250 degrees to cook the dough for any Roman-style pizza recipes, which require the dough.

GLUTEN-FREE PIZZA DOUGH

PREPARATION
120 min

COOKING
10-20 min

SERVES
2

INGREDIENTS

- 1 cup lukewarm water
- ¼ cup whole milk, at room temperature
- 1 tablespoon plus 2 teaspoons active dry yeast
- 1 extra-large egg
- 5¼ cups gluten-free flour
- 2 teaspoons baking powder, sifted
- 2 teaspoons kosher salt
- 2 teaspoons sugar
- 2 tablespoons extra-virgin olive oil, divided

DIRECTIONS

1. In a small bowl, combine the warm water and milk. Sprinkle the yeast evenly over the surface and stir to combine. Set aside in a warm spot until active and bubbly, about 15 minutes.

2. When the yeast mixture is active and bubbly, lightly whisk in the egg.

3. Attach the paddle to your stand mixer. In the work bowl, combine the flour, baking powder, salt, and sugar and mix on low speed.

4. Add the bubbly sponge to the work bowl and mix on low speed until combined, 2 to 3 minutes.

5. Gather the dough and transfer to a not floured work surface. Briefly knead the dough to combine, 4 or 5 turns total.

6. Divide the dough into two equal portions and wrap each tightly in plastic wrap. Gently shape each into a 2-inch-thick disc. Leave to rise in a warm spot for 45 minutes.

7. Preheat the wood oven to approximately 500°F. Brush a quarter sheet pan with 1 tablespoon of the olive oil.

8. Using a wooden rolling pin, roll out the dough on a clean, dry, not floured surface to ¼-inch thickness, and transfer to the prepared sheet pan. With a sharp paring knife, trim away any excess dough that hangs over the sides of the tray. Fill in any gaps by using the trimmed pieces, pressing the seams together. The entire tray should be filled to the edges. With the tines of a fork, prick the entire surface of the dough.

9. Brush the remaining 1-tablespoon of olive oil over the top of the dough. Transfer to a warm spot and allow the dough to proof for 15 minutes before baking.

10. Bake the dough in a relatively cool zone of the oven, away from the fire, until lightly browned, 8 to 10 minutes, making sure to rotate frequently. Remove the tray from the oven and leave to cool slightly. Add the toppings of your choice and return to the hot oven and bake until warmed through, about 5 minutes more.

SPELT PIZZA DOUGH

PREPARATION
15 min

COOKING
40 min

SERVINGS
4

INGREDIENTS

- 2 tbsp. honey
- 1 tbsp. extra virgin olive oil
- 1 tsp. kosher salt
- 1 package active dry yeast
- 3 cups sprouted spelt flour
- 1 cup warm water

DIRECTIONS

1. In a bowl, whisk water, yeast, honey, and 1 cup of flour together. Let it stand for about 20 minutes until the mixture is bubbly and the yeast softens.

2. In a bowl, beat the mixture that has remained using an electric mixer that has been fitted with a dough hook attachment and if necessary, adding more flour until a tacky and soft dough is formed. This takes 3-4 minutes.

3. Put the dough in a mixing bowl with some olive oil and use a plate to cover the bowl and let the dough rise and dough in size, this takes like 1 hour 30 minutes.

4. Transfer the dough to a lightly floured work surface after punching it. Divide the dough into 4 balls and leave each to rest after it's covered until the dough slightly rises for like 30 to 45 minutes.

5. Finally, roll them into the desired thickness and shapes.

CLASSIC THIN CRUST PIZZA DOUGH

PREPARATION
15 min

COOKING
60 min

SERVINGS
4

INGREDIENTS

- 2 tablespoons dry active yeast
- 1 cup lukewarm water
- 4 cups flour
- 2 tablespoons extra virgin olive oil
- 1 ½ teaspoons salt

DIRECTIONS

1. In a large bowl, dissolve the yeast in the water.
2. Combine the flour, oil, and salt.
3. Then stir the flour into the yeast mixture in small batches. The dough should start to become smooth and pull away from the sides of the bowl. If it doesn't, adjust water and flour amounts as necessary.
4. Cover your work surface with a dusting of flour and quickly knead the dough until it becomes elastic and easy to work with.
5. Oil a clean bowl and place the dough in it; cover with lightly oiled plastic wrap.
6. Allow the dough to rise in a warm spot for 1 to 3 hours or until it has doubled in size.

MEAT

PARMESAN PORK CHOPS WITH PARMESAN

PREPARATION
10 min

COOKING
15 min

SERVINGS
6

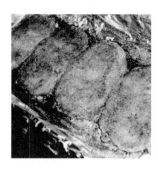

INGREDIENTS

- 1 tablespoon salt
- 1 teaspoon ground black pepper
- 1 teaspoon chili flakes
- 2-pound pork loin
- 1 cup breadcrumbs
- 2 tablespoon Italian spices
- 3 tablespoon olive oil
- 5 oz Parmesan

DIRECTIONS

1. Slice the pork loin into the serving chops.
2. Then rub the pork chops with the salt and ground black pepper.
3. Add chili flakes.
4. Then combine the breadcrumbs with Italian spices and stir the mixture with the help of the fork.
5. After this grate Parmesan cheese.
6. Pour the olive oil into the pan.
7. Add the grated cheese to the breadcrumbs mixture and stir it.
8. Coat the pork chops in the breadcrumb's mixture carefully.
9. Roast the pork chops in the preheated olive oil for 10 minutes totally from both sides.
10. Then chill the cooked pork chops.

SUNDAY GRAVY

PREPARATION
15 min

COOKING
40 min

SERVINGS
4

INGREDIENTS

- 3 tbsp. olive oil
- 2 lb. beef ribs
- 3 oxtails
- 3 pork chops
- 1/4 cup grated Parmigiano-Reggiano cheese
- 1 lb. Italian sausages
- ½ lb. neck bones
- 1 diced onion
- 4 minced garlic cloves
- 2 28 oz. crushed tomatoes
- 2 cups tomato sauce
- 2 cups water, divided
- 1/4 cup tomato paste
- 1 tbsp. chopped basil
- 1 tsp. oregano
- Salt and pepper to taste

DIRECTIONS

1. First, preheat your oven to 425 degrees.
2. Place all the meat on a roasting pan and drizzle with 2 tbsp. olive oil 3. Roast the meat for 30 minutes.
3. Heat 1 tbsp. oil in a large pot. Then, sauté the onion for 5 minutes.
4. Next, add the garlic. Sauté for 1 minute 6. Season with salt and pepper.
5. Then, stir in the tomato and tomato sauce, along with all the roast meat.
6. Stir well to combine.
7. Add the tomato paste, herbs, and cheese.
8. Then, simmer for 4 hours.
9. Adjust seasoning to taste

CLASSIC LASAGNA BEEF

PREPARATION
15 min

COOKING
55 min

SERVES
8

INGREDIENTS

- 1 teaspoon paprika
- 1 teaspoon salt
- ½ cup tomato sauce
- 5 oz Mozzarella
- 1 cup chicken stock
- 14 oz minced beef
- 1 teaspoon minced garlic
- 8 oz lasagna sheets
- 1 teaspoon oregano
- 3 tablespoon olive oil
- ½ teaspoon nutmeg

DIRECTIONS

1. Combine the minced beef with the paprika, oregano, salt, and nutmeg.
2. Add the minced garlic and mix the mixture up.
3. After this, pour the olive oil into the pan and add the minced beef mixture.
4. Add the tomato sauce and stir the mixture with the help of the spatula.
5. After this, simmer the sauce for 10 minutes on the medium heat.
6. Grate Mozzarella.
7. Preheat the oven to 360 F.
8. Put 1 lasagna sheet on the bottom of the form.
9. After this, spread this sheet with the cooked minced beef sauce.
10. Sprinkle it with the small amount of the grated cheese and put the second lasagna sheet over the mass.
11. Repeat the steps till the last lasagna sheet.
12. Sprinkle the last lasagna sheet with the grated cheese generously.
13. Pour the chicken stock in the form and place the lasagna in the preheated oven.
14. Cook the dish for 40 minutes.
15. Serve the lasagna hot.

ITALIAN CALZONE CHEESE

PREPARATION
20 min

COOKING
25 min

SERVES
9

INGREDIENTS

- 3 cup flour
- 1 teaspoon salt
- 1 cup ricotta cheese
- 8 oz Cheddar cheese
- 7 oz pepperoni
- 1 teaspoon fresh yeast
- 7 oz water
- ½ teaspoon sugar
- 1 tablespoon olive oil
- 1 cup mushrooms
- 1 egg
- 1 tablespoon butter

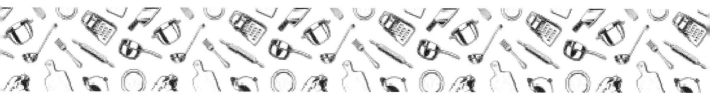

DIRECTIONS

1. Preheat the water little to make it warm.
2. Then add the fresh yeast in the warm water and stir it carefully till the yeast is dissolved.
3. After this, add sugar and salt.
4. Sift the flour into the mixture and add olive oil.
5. Knead the smooth and non-sticky dough.
6. Cover the dough with the towel and place it in the warm place to rise.
7. Meanwhile, shred Cheddar cheese and slice the mushrooms.
8. Chop pepperoni.
9. Beat the egg in the bowl and whisk it.
10. Add the chopped pepperoni and shredded cheese in the whisked egg.
11. Make the butter soft and add it to the filling mixture. Mix it up well.
12. Roll the raised dough and make the thin circles with the help of the cutter.
13. Then put the tablespoon of the filling in the middle of the dough circle and secure the dough.
14. Preheat the oven to 355 F.
15. Cover the tray with the baking paper or parchment.
16. Put the calzone on the tray and transfer the tray to the oven.
17. Bake the dish for 25 minutes.
18. Serve the cooked calzone hot.

ITALIAN MEAT TORTE CHEESE

PREPARATION
15 min

COOKING
40 min

SERVES
8

INGREDIENTS

- 10 oz Provolone
- 8 oz ham
- 9 oz Cheddar cheese
- 10 oz yeast dough
- 6 oz prosciutto
- 8 eggs
- 1 tablespoon butter

DIRECTIONS

1. Cut the yeast dough into 4 similar parts.
2. Then roll the yeast parts in the shape of the round baking form.
3. Spread the baking form with the butter.
4. Cut the ham and prosciutto into the strips.
5. Beat the eggs in the bowl and whisk them.
6. Grate Cheddar cheese and Provolone cheese.
7. Put the first part of the rolled yeast dough in the form.
8. Sprinkle it with the grated Cheddar cheese.
9. Add the layer of ham and prosciutto.
10. Sprinkle the dish with a small amount of Provolone cheese.
11. Place the second part of the dough over the cheese and repeat all the steps.
12. You should use all the filling for the third rolled dough piece.
13. Cover the torte with the last rolled dough pieces and sprinkle it with the whisked eggs.
14. Preheat the oven to 365 F and put the torte there.
15. Cook the dish for 40 minutes.
16. When the torte is cooked – it will have a golden-brown crust.
17. Cut the torte into the serving pieces.

ZITI WITH SAUSAGE

PREPARATION
15 min

COOKING
40 min

SERVINGS
4

INGREDIENTS

- 1 lb. crumbled Italian sausage
- 1 cup sliced mushrooms
- ½ cup diced celery
- 1 diced onion
- 3 minced garlic cloves
- 42 oz. store-bought spaghetti sauce or homemade
- Salt and pepper to taste
- ½ tsp. oregano
- ½ tsp. basil
- 1 lb. uncooked ziti pasta
- 1 cup shredded mozzarella cheese
- ½ cup grated parmesan cheese
- 3 tbsp. chopped parsley

DIRECTIONS

1. Brown the sausage, mushrooms, onion, and celery in a skillet for 5 minutes.
2. Next, stir in the garlic. Then, cook for 3 more minutes. Set aside.
3. Using another skillet, add the spaghetti sauce, salt, pepper, oregano, and basil.
4. Let the sauce simmer for 15 minutes.
5. While the sauce cooks, prepare the pasta in a pan according to directions. Drain.
6. Preheat the oven to 350 degrees.
7. In a baking dish create two layers of ziti, sausage mixture, and shredded mozzarella.
8. Then, sprinkle the top with parsley and parmesan cheese.
9. Bake for 25 minutes.

SAUSAGE AND PEPPERS

PREPARATION
15 min

COOKING
50 min

SERVINGS
4

INGREDIENTS

- 1 package spaghetti
- 1 tbsp. olive oil
- 3 minced garlic cloves
- 1 tsp. Italian seasoning
- Salt and pepper to taste
- 3 tbsp. virgin olive oil
- 12 oz. canned diced tomatoes
- 3 tbsp. red wine
- 1/3 cup chopped parsley
- ¼ cup grated Asiago cheese

DIRECTIONS

1. Cook the spaghetti according to directions, about 5 minutes. Drain 2. Heat the olive oil in a skillet and brown the sausages for 5 minutes.
2. Transfer the sausage to a plate.
3. To the same skillet, add the peppers, garlic, Italian seasoning, salt, and pepper.
4. Drizzle the peppers with 3 tbsp. olive oil.
5. Stir in the diced tomatoes and wine.
6. Sauté for 10 minutes.
7. Toss the pasta with the peppers and adjust the seasoning.
8. Top with parsley and Asiago cheese.

SAUCY LASAGNA

PREPARATION
15 min

COOKING
40 min

SERVES
4

INGREDIENTS

- 1 ½ lb. crumbled spicy Italian sausage
- 5 cups store-bought spaghetti sauce or any of the recipe sauces in this book
- 1 cup tomato sauce
- 1 tsp Italian seasoning
- ½ cup red wine
- 1 tbsp. sugar
- 1 tbsp. oil
- 5 minced garlic gloves
- 1 diced onion
- 1 cup shredded mozzarella cheese
- 1 cup shredded provolone cheese
- 2 cups ricotta cheese
- 1 cup cottage cheese
- 2 large eggs
- ¼ cup milk
- 9 noodles lasagna noodles – parboil them for about 5 minutes
- ¼ cup grated parmesan cheese

DIRECTIONS

1. Preheat the oven to 375 degrees.
2. Brown the crumbled sausage in a skillet for 5 minutes. Discard any grease.
3. Place the pasta sauce, tomato sauce, and Italian seasoning, red wine, and sugar in a large pot and stir well.
4. Heat the olive oil in a skillet. Then, sauté the garlic and onion for 5 minutes.
5. Stir the sausage and sautéed garlic and onion into the sauce.
6. Next, cover the pot and simmer for 45 minutes.
7. Stir together the mozzarella and provolone cheese in a bowl.
8. Combine the ricotta, cottage cheese, eggs, and milk in another bowl.
9. Using a 9 x 13 baking dish, cover the bottom of the dish with ½ cup of sauce.
10. Next, fill the baking dish by creating 3 separate layers: noodles, sauce, ricotta, and mozzarella.
11. Dust the top with parmesan cheese.
12. Bake for 30 minutes in a covered dish.
13. Uncover the dish and bake for another 15 minutes.

TRADITIONAL MEATLOAF UNO

PREPARATION
15 min

COOKING
35 min

SERVES
10

INGREDIENTS

- 1 teaspoon ground black pepper
- ½ teaspoon paprika
- 1 onion
- 6 oz Parmesan
- 1 cup tomato paste
- 1 tablespoon tomato puree
- 3-pound ground beef
- 4 eggs
- ½ cup breadcrumbs
- 1 teaspoon salt
- 1 teaspoon cayenne pepper
- 1 tablespoon olive oil
- 5 oz carrot
- ½ tablespoon kosher salt
- 1 teaspoon sugar

DIRECTIONS

1. Beat the egg in the bowl and whisk them with the help of the hand whisker.
2. After this, add salt, ground black pepper, paprika, and breadcrumbs.
3. Add the ground beef and mix the mixture gently.
4. Then grate Parmesan cheese and peel the onion.
5. Grate the onion and add the meatloaf mass.
6. Add the grated cheese and stir it carefully.
7. Put the meatloaf mass in the loaf form.
8. Place the meatloaf in the oven and cook it in the preheated to 365 F oven for 35 minutes.
9. Meanwhile, make the sauce: combine the tomato paste and tomato puree together and pour the liquid into the saucepan.
10. Add cayenne pepper and olive oil.
11. Peel the carrot and grate it into the saucepan with the tomato sauce liquid.
12. Add sugar and kosher salt and mix it.
13. Close the lid and simmer the dish on the medium heat for 20 minutes. Stir the sauce frequently.
14. When the meatloaf is cooked – remove it from the oven and discard from the form.
15. Slice the meatloaf and sprinkle it with the cooked sauce.
16. Serve the dish with the separated bowl of the remaining tomato sauce.

NEW ITALIAN STEAK

PREPARATION
25 min

COOKING
10 min

SERVINGS
3

INGREDIENTS

- ¼ teaspoon ground ginger
- 1 tablespoon olive oil
- 3 tablespoon tomato puree
- 1 teaspoon Italian spices
- 16 oz beef steak
- 1 tablespoon garlic, grated
- 1 teaspoon cayenne pepper
- 1 teaspoon kosher salt
- 1 tablespoon honey

DIRECTIONS

1. Combine the grated garlic with the olive oil and honey.
2. Whisk the mixture well.
3. Combine the cayenne pepper, ground ginger, Italian spices, kosher salt, and tomato puree. Whisk the mixture.
4. Then coat the beef steaks with the tomato mixture and leave for 10 minutes to marinate.
5. Meanwhile, preheat the grill well.
6. When the time of marinating is over – remove the beef steaks from the tomato sauce.
7. Brush the beef steak with the olive oil mixture.
8. Then put the beef steaks on the grill and grill them for 4 minutes from each side.
9. Pin the meat and check if there is no remaining blood.
10. If the blood exists – cook the beefsteak for 4 minutes more.
11. Serve Italian steaks immediately.

BEEF CARPACCIO SPECIAL

PREPARATION
10 min

COOKING
40 min

SERVINGS
4

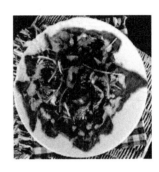

INGREDIENTS

- 1 teaspoon ground black pepper
- 3 tablespoon mustard
- 2 egg yolks
- 17 oz beef tenderloin
- 1 cup arugula
- 5 tablespoon olive oil
- 1 teaspoon salt
- 4 tablespoon lemon juice
- 4 tomatoes

DIRECTIONS

1. Put the beef tenderloin in the freezer and freeze it for 2-3 hours.
2. Meanwhile, tear the arugula.
3. Combine the salt and ground black pepper together.
4. Whisk the egg yolks with the mustard and lemon juice.
5. Add olive oil and continue to whisk the mixture till you get the lemon color light sauce.
6. Then remove the frozen beef tenderloin from the freezer and slice into the thin slices with the help of the sharp knife.
7. Put the sliced beef into the big serving plate.
8. Sprinkle the meat with the salt-pepper mixture.
9. After this, sprinkle the dish with the mustard light sauce.
10. Add the arugula and sprinkle the dish with the olive oil.
11. Serve the carpaccio immediately.

MANICOTTI PORK

PREPARATION
20 min

COOKING
35 min

SERVES
8

INGREDIENTS

- 12 manicottis
- 1 cup milk
- 1 cup ricotta
- 7 oz Mozzarella
- 7 oz Parmesan
- 1 tablespoon fresh basil
- 1 teaspoon cilantro
- 1 teaspoon thyme
- 4 oz white onion
- 1 tablespoon olive oil
- 9 oz ground pork
- 1 teaspoon ground black pepper
- 1 teaspoon salt
- 1 teaspoon minced garlic
- 3 tablespoon tomato sauce
- 4 tablespoon butter

DIRECTIONS

1. Put the manicotti on the tray and transfer the tray to the oven.
2. Bake the manicotti for 5 minutes.
3. Meanwhile, combine the ground pork and olive oil in the big saucepan.
4. Add ground black pepper, salt, fresh basil, cilantro, thyme, minced garlic, and tomato sauce.
5. Peel the onion and dice it.
6. Add the diced onion to the ground beef mixture.
7. Add butter and simmer the ground beef mixture for 15 minutes or till all the ingredients are cooked.
8. After this, combine the ricotta and milk together.
9. Whisk the mixture.
10. Chop Parmesan cheese and Mozzarella cheese.
11. Add the chopped cheese in the whisked milk mixture.
12. Chill manicotti well and place 1 manicotti in the form.
13. Sprinkle it with the cooked ground beef mixture.
14. Repeat the same step with all the manicotti.
15. After this, cover the last manicotti with the remaining ground beef mixture and pour the milk mixture.
16. Transfer the unprepared dish in the oven and cook it for 25 minutes.
17. When the manicotti has the golden-brown color of the crust – it is cooked.

GREAT ITALIAN BEEF

PREPARATION
15 min

COOKING
90 min

SERVES
9

INGREDIENTS

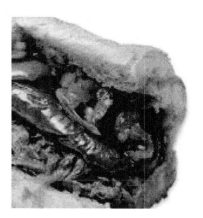

- 3 tablespoon minced garlic
- 1 chili pepper
- 15 oz beef, sliced, roasted
- 1 teaspoon salt
- 1 teaspoon ground black pepper
- 21 oz beef neck
- 10 oz oxtail
- 7 oz onion
- 1 oz bay leaf
- 1 carrot
- 1 teaspoon ground clove
- 12 cup water
- 10 oz Italian rolls

DIRECTIONS

1. Preheat the oven to 450 F.
2. Then trim as much meat as possible from the beef neck and oxtails.
3. Put the bones and trimmed meat in the tray.
4. Add sliced beef and transfer the mixture to the oven.
5. Cook it for 30 minutes. Turn the meat into sides from time to time.
6. Peel the carrot and onion.
7. Slice the carrot and chop the onion.
8. After 30 minutes – remove the fat from the tray with meat and leave only 3 tablespoons of fat there.
9. Add the sliced carrot and chopped onion.
10. Add the bay leaf, salt, and ground black pepper.
11. After this, add ground clove and pour the water.
12. Return the tray back in the oven and cook it for 20 minutes more.
13. Meanwhile, chop chili pepper and combine it with the minced garlic.
14. Preheat the pan and roast the chili mixture for 1 minute. Stir it constantly.
15. When the meat is cooked – remove the tray from the oven and transfer the beef broth into the saucepan.
16. Take only 1 cup of the beef broth and add the chili mixture in it.
17. Start to preheat it on the medium heat.
18. Chop all the cooked beef and transfer it to the boiled beef broth.
19. Simmer the dish for 10 minutes on the medium heat.
20. Then cut Italian rolls crosswise.
21. Put the meat mixture in the rolls and wrap them in the foil.
22. Transfer the rolls in the preheated to 350 F oven and cook for 7 minutes more.
23. Serve the hot dish immediately.

BEEF MEATBALLS

PREPARATION
15 min

COOKING
25 min

SERVINGS
8

INGREDIENTS

- 1 teaspoon ground black pepper
- 2 tablespoon semolina
- 1 tablespoon butter
- 3-pound ground beef
- ½ cup fresh dill
- 10 oz Parmesan
- 1 teaspoon kosher salt
- 1 teaspoon oregano
- 1 teaspoon chili flakes
- 1 cup breadcrumbs
- 1 teaspoon marinara sauce

DIRECTIONS

1. Combine the ground beef with the semolina and ground black pepper.
2. Add kosher salt and oregano.
3. After this, sprinkle the forcemeat with the chili flakes.
4. Chop the fresh dill and add to the meat mixture.
5. Mix the ground beef mixture carefully.
6. Grate Parmesan cheese and combine it with the breadcrumbs.
7. Make the medium oval meatballs from the beef mixture and coat them in the cheese mass.
8. Preheat the oven to 365 F.
9. Put the meatballs on the covered with the parchment tray and put the tray in the oven.
10. Bake the dish for 25 minutes.
11. Stir the meatballs into the second side once during the cooking.
12. When the beef meatballs are cooked – transfer them to the serving bowl and sprinkle with the marinara sauce gently.

ITALIAN CHILI BEEF

PREPARATION
15 min

COOKING
45 min

SERVINGS
8

INGREDIENTS

- 1 onion
- 1 teaspoon ground black pepper
- 1 teaspoon coriander
- 1 teaspoon basil
- 1/3 cup beef broth
- 1 cup red beans, cooked
- 1 zucchini
- 3-pound ground beef
- 1 cup tomato puree
- 1 teaspoon salt
- 1 teaspoon minced garlic
- 1 cup bell pepper
- 2 tablespoon olive oil
- 1 cup mushrooms
- ½ cup tomato paste

DIRECTIONS

1. Chop zucchini and onion into the same pieces.
2. Pour the tomato puree and tomato paste in the saucepan.
3. Add minced garlic, salt, ground black pepper, coriander, basil, and mix the mixture.
4. After this, add ground beef and sauté the dish for 15 minutes on the medium heat.
5. After this, add zucchini and onion.
6. Add olive oil and beef broth.
7. Chop the bell pepper and add it to the saucepan too.
8. Mix the chili carefully with the help of the wooden spatula and add red beans.
9. Close the lid and cook the chili for 15 minutes more.
10. When the time is over – check if all the ingredients of the chili are tender.
11. Serve the dish immediately or let to rest for 10 minutes.

ITALIAN SLIDERS

PREPARATION
20 min

COOKING
15 min

SERVES
8

INGREDIENTS

- 12 oz ham
- 10 oz pepperoni
- 9 oz salami
- 2 red pepper
- 1 tablespoon olive oil
- 10 oz Hawaii Sweet rolls
- 7 oz butter
- 2 tablespoon fresh parsley
- 7 oz Parmesan cheese
- 5 tablespoon garlic sauce

DIRECTIONS

1. Discard the seeds from the red peppers and chop them.
2. Pour the olive oil into the pan and add chopped red peppers.
3. Roast the red peppers for 3 minutes on the medium heat. Stir the vegetables frequently.
4. Slice the ham and pepperoni.
5. After this, slice the salami.
6. Chop the fresh parsley and grate Parmesan cheese.
7. Slice Hawaii Sweet rolls into 2 parts.
8. Preheat the oven to 360 F.
9. Then rub the 2 parts of Hawaii Sweet rolls with the butter. Leave 1 teaspoon of the butter for spreading the form.
10. Sprinkle the rolls with the small amount grated cheese.
11. After this, spread the form with the butter.
12. After this, put the bottom part of the rolls in the form.
13. Then make the layer of the sliced ham.
14. Sprinkle the rolls with the grated cheese.
15. After this, make the layer of the pepperoni and sprinkle the dish with the roasted red pepper.
16. Then put the fresh parsley and salami.
17. Sprinkle the dish with the garlic sauce.
18. Sprinkle the rolls with the remaining grated cheese and cover with the second part of the rolls.
19. Put the slider in the preheated oven and cook the dish for 15 minutes.
20. Then remove the cooked dish from the oven and chill for 3 minutes.

MEAT PORCHETTA

PREPARATION
15 min

COOKING
130 min

SERVINGS
8

INGREDIENTS

- 1 tablespoon chili flakes
- 1 tablespoon minced garlic
- 1 teaspoon rosemary
- 15 oz pork belly
- 10 oz pork loin
- 1 tablespoon fennel seeds
- 1 teaspoon salt

DIRECTIONS

1. Rub the pork loin with the minced garlic, rosemary, and salt.
2. After this, put the pork loin on the pork belly. Roll the meat.
3. Put the fennel seeds and chili flakes in the pan and roast them for 2 minutes on the high heat.
4. Then sprinkle the rolled pork belly with the roasted spices and coat it with the foil.
5. Preheat the oven to 400 F and put Porchetta in the oven and cook it for 2 hours.
6. Then discard the foil and cook Porchetta for 10 minutes more.
7. Then chill the cooked dish very well.
8. Slice it into the serving pieces.

CHICKEN

CARAMELIZED CHICKEN

PREPARATION
10 min

COOKING
35 min

SERVES
8

INGREDIENTS

- 3 tablespoon water
- 2-pound chicken breast, skinless, boneless
- 3 garlic cloves
- 1 teaspoon olive oil
- 1 tablespoon liquid honey
- 1 teaspoon cayenne pepper
- 1 teaspoon chili flakes
- ½ cup sugar
- 1 teaspoon cilantro
- 1 tablespoon garlic sauce
- 1 tablespoon basil

DIRECTIONS

1. Rub the chicken breast with the cayenne pepper, chili pepper, cilantro, garlic sauce, and basil.
2. Wrap the chicken breast in the foil.
3. Preheat the oven to 365 F and put the wrapped chicken breast there.
4. Cook the chicken for 25 minutes.
5. Then pour the water into the deep saucepan.
6. Add sugar and liquid honey.
7. Simmer the mixture on the medium heat until you get thick caramel.
8. Then remove the chicken from the oven and discard the foil.
9. Transfer the chicken breast in the caramel and coat it well.
10. Close the lid and roast the chicken on the high heat for 2 minutes.
11. Then open the lid and turn it to the second side. Roast the chicken breast for 2 minutes more.
12. Remove the chicken breast from the heat and let it rest for 10 minutes.
13. Then slice the chicken breast and sprinkle it with the remaining caramel.

BBQ CHICKEN

PREPARATION
20 min

COOKING
14 min

SERVINGS
6

INGREDIENTS

- 15 oz chicken breast
- 9 tablespoon BBQ sauce
- 1 tablespoon minced garlic
- 2 cups Italian dressing

DIRECTIONS

1. Combine Italian dressing with the BBQ sauce and minced garlic.
2. Mix the mixture up.
3. Then put the chicken breasts in the BBQ mixture and coat them well.
4. Leave the meat for 15 minutes to marinate.
5. Meanwhile, preheat the grill to 365 F.
6. When the chicken breasts are marinated – transfer them to the preheated grill.
7. Grill the chicken breast for 7 minutes on each side.
8. Serve the cooked meal immediately.

HONEY ITALIAN CHICKEN STRIPS

PREPARATION
10 min

COOKING
20 min

SERVINGS
8

INGREDIENTS

- 1 teaspoon paprika
- 1 teaspoon chili flakes
- 3 tablespoon olive oil
- 1 teaspoon onion powder
- ½ cup flour
- 2 tablespoon liquid honey
- 1 teaspoon thyme
- ½ teaspoon basil
- 1 teaspoon oregano
- 14 oz chicken fillet
- 1 cup ricotta

DIRECTIONS

1. Put the thyme, basil, oregano, paprika, chili flakes, and onion powder in the big bowl.
2. Add the flour and stir the mixture.
3. After this, cut the chicken fillet into the strips.
4. Coat the chicken strips with the flour-herb mixture.
5. Pour the olive oil into the pan and preheat it.
6. Toss the chicken strips in the preheated oil and roast the chicken strips for 10 minutes on the medium heat.
7. After this, add ricotta cheese and simmer the chicken for 3 minutes more.
8. Pour the liquid honey in the separated pan and melt it.
9. Then add the chicken strips in the honey and stir the dish.
10. Remove the chicken strips from the heat and leave them for 7 minutes.
11. After this, serve the dish.

ITALIAN CHICKEN SPIEDINI

PREPARATION
10 min

COOKING
12 min

SERVINGS
4

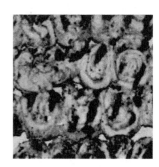

INGREDIENTS

- 1 teaspoon fresh dill
- 1 tablespoon lemon zest
- 1 teaspoon minced garlic
- 3 tablespoon basil oil
- 1-pound chicken fillet
- 6 oz Italian breadcrumbs
- 4 oz Parmesan cheese
- 1 tablespoon butter

DIRECTIONS

1. Slice the chicken fillet into the thin pieces.
2. Grate Parmesan cheese.
3. Combine the fresh dill, breadcrumbs, lemon zest, and minced garlic together.
4. Stir the mixture carefully until it starts to be homogenous.
5. After this, coat the chicken pieces with the breadcrumb's mixture carefully.
6. Roll the chicken pieces and secure them with the wooden sticks.
7. Thread on the chicken rolls on the metal skewers and remove the wooden sticks.
8. After this, sprinkle the chicken with the basil oil and butter.
9. Preheat the grill to 365 F and put the chicken spiedini there.
10. Cook it for 4 minutes from each side.
11. After this, sprinkle the chicken with the grated cheese and cook it until Parmesan starts to melt.
12. Serve the cook chicken spiedini immediately.

GARLIC CHEDDAR CHICKEN

PREPARATION
15 min

COOKING
40 min

SERVINGS
4

INGREDIENTS

- ¼ cup butter
- ¼ cup olive oil
- ½ cup grated parmesan cheese
- ½ cup Panko breadcrumbs
- ½ cup crushed Ritz crackers
- 3 minced garlic cloves
- 1 ¼ sharp cheddar cheese
- ¼ tsp. Italian seasoning
- Salt and pepper to taste
- ¼ cup flour
- 8 chicken breasts

DIRECTIONS

1. Preheat the oven to 350 degrees.
2. Heat the butter and olive oil in your skillet and sauté the garlic for 5 minutes.
3. Combine the breadcrumbs, crushed crackers, both cheeses, seasoning, salt, and pepper in a bowl.
4. Quickly dip each piece of chicken into the butter/olive oil mixture.
5. Dredge the chicken through the flour.
6. Coat the chicken with the breadcrumb mixture.
7. Transfer each chicken piece to a baking dish.
8. Top with a drizzling of the butter/oil mixture.
9. Bake for 30 minutes 10. Place under the broiler for 2 minutes for some extra crispiness.

CHICKEN FETTUCCINI ALFREDO

PREPARATION
15 min

COOKING
30 min

SERVINGS
4

INGREDIENTS

- 1 lb. fettuccine pasta
- 6 boneless, skinless chicken breasts, nicely cut into cubes
- ¾ cup butter, divided
- 5 minced garlic cloves
- 1 tsp. thyme
- 1 tsp. oregano
- 1 diced onion
- 1 cup sliced mushrooms
- ½ cup flour
- Salt and pepper to taste
- 3 cups full milk
- 1 cup heavy cream
- ¼ cup grated gruyere cheese
- ¾ cup grated parmesan cheese-get fresh parmesan and grate it yourself.
- It makes all the difference.

DIRECTIONS

1. 1. Cook for pasta according to directions, about 10 minutes, and set aside.
2. 2. Melt 2 tbsp. butter in your skillet and stir in the chicken cubes, garlic, thyme, and oregano and cook on low for 5 minutes, until the chicken is no longer pink. Set aside.
3. 3. Melt the remaining 4 tbsp. butter in the skillet and sauté the onion, and mushrooms.
4. 4. Next, add the flour, salt, pepper, and stir for 3 minutes.
5. 5. Pour in the milk and heavy cream. Then, stir for 2 minutes.
6. 6. Add the cheese and stir for 3 minutes on low.
7. 7. Then, return the chicken to the skillet, adjust the seasoning.
8. 8. Cook on low for 3 minutes.
9. 9. Serve over the pasta.

MOZZARELLA CHICKEN TIGHTS

PREPARATION
20 min

COOKING
25 min

SERVINGS
6

INGREDIENTS

- 1 teaspoon cilantro
- 2-pound chicken tights
- 1 teaspoon rosemary
- 1 tablespoon butter
- 1 teaspoon olive oil
- 3 tablespoon tomato sauce
- 1 tablespoon minced garlic
- ½ cup cream
- 1 teaspoon paprika
- 8 oz Mozzarella
- 1 teaspoon lemon juice

DIRECTIONS

1. Combine the tomato sauce and minced garlic together and whisk the mixture.
2. After this, rub the chicken tights with the tomato sauce mixture.
3. Combine paprika and cilantro.
4. After this, add rosemary and lemon juice. Stir the mixture until it is homogenous.
5. Then add olive oil.
6. Sprinkle the chicken tights with the spice mixture and leave it for 10 minutes more to rest.
7. Then slice Mozzarella.
8. Pour the cream into the baking form and add the chicken tights.
9. Then add butter and make the layer from sliced Mozzarella.
10. Bake the chicken for 25 minutes at 360 F.
11. When the time is over, and chicken is cooked – serve it immediately.

TRADITIONAL ITALIAN CHICKEN

PREPARATION
15 min

COOKING
45 min

SERVES
9

INGREDIENTS

- 1 teaspoon chili flakes
- 1 teaspoon onion powder
- ¼ cup flour
- 3 tablespoon olive oil
- 1 teaspoon cilantro
- 1 teaspoon thyme
- 3 tomatoes
- 1 cup tomato paste
- 3-pound chicken
- 1 tablespoon oregano
- 1 tablespoon basil
- 1 tablespoon paprika
- 1 cup chicken stock
- 8 oz Mozzarella

DIRECTIONS

1. Put the oregano, basil, paprika, chili flakes, onion powder, and flour in the big plastic bag.
2. Shake the mixture.
3. After this, chop the chicken roughly and add to the spice mixture bag.
4. Close the bag and shake it well.
5. Pour the olive oil into the pan and make it hot.
6. Then toss the chicken mixture in the hot oil and roast it for 3 minutes on the high heat.
7. Stir the chicken from time to time.
8. Meanwhile, slice Mozzarella and tomatoes.
9. Pour the chicken stock into the form and make the layer of the sliced tomatoes.
10. After this, sprinkle the sliced tomatoes with the thyme and cilantro.
11. Transfer the roasted chicken in the form too.
12. Sprinkle the chicken with the remaining liquid from the pan.
13. Then make the layer of the sliced cheese over the chicken.
14. Preheat the oven to 365 F.
15. Cover the surface of the form with the foil and transfer the form in the oven.
16. Bake the chicken for 40 minutes.
17. Then serve the cooked meal immediately.

CHICKEN CUTLETS

PREPARATION
10 min

COOKING
15 min

SERVINGS
9

INGREDIENTS

- 1 teaspoon ground black pepper
- 1 teaspoon turmeric
- 1 teaspoon paprika
- ½ teaspoon chili flakes
- 1 onion
- 15 oz ground chicken
- 1 tablespoon dried dill
- 1 cup Panko breadcrumbs
- ½ cup ricotta
- 1/3 cup Italian parsley
- 14 tablespoon butter
- 1 teaspoon minced garlic
- 1 teaspoon rosemary
- 1 teaspoon sage
- 1 egg

DIRECTIONS

1. Combine the ground chicken with the breadcrumbs and ricotta.
2. Beat the egg in the mixture and sprinkle with the ground black pepper, turmeric, paprika, chili flakes, and dried dill.
3. Peel the onion and grate it.
4. Combine the grated onion with the minced garlic and add the mixture to the cutlet mass.
5. Add sage and knead the ground chicken dough.
6. Toss the butter in the pan and preheat it.
7. Add the rosemary and roast it for 1 minute.
8. After this, discard the rosemary.
9. Make the round cutlets from the chicken mixture and put them in the pan.
10. Roast the cutlets for 5 minutes on each side.
11. When all the cutlets are cooked – serve them.

CHICKEN SKILLET RICOTTA

PREPARATION
15 min

COOKING
40 min

SERVINGS
14

INGREDIENTS

- 1 onion
- 3 oz garlic
- 1 tablespoon onion powder
- 1 teaspoon salt
- 3 tablespoon olive oil
- ½ cup ricotta
- 10 oz chicken tights
- 10 oz chicken wings
- 10 oz chicken drumsticks
- 1 teaspoon chili flakes
- 1 teaspoon ground black pepper

DIRECTIONS

1. Peel the onion and garlic cloves.
2. Slice the vegetables.
3. Combine the onion powder, salt, ground black pepper, and chili flakes in the shallow bowl.
4. Stir the spices with the help of the fork.
5. After this, put all the chicken in the big bowl and sprinkle it with the spice mixture.
6. Mix the chicken carefully with the help of the fingertips.
7. After this, add the sliced onion and garlic and mix the chicken carefully again.
8. Then sprinkle the meat with the ricotta and olive oil.
9. Toss the chicken mixture in the skillet.
10. Cook the dish for 40 minutes. Stir the chicken frequently.
11. Serve the prepared chicken in the skillet.

ITALIAN-STYLE KABOBS CHICKEN

PREPARATION
25 min

COOKING
7 min

SERVINGS
5

INGREDIENTS

- ½ cup Italian parsley
- 1 tablespoon olive oil
- 1 teaspoon ground black pepper
- 2-pound chicken breast, boneless
- 1 tablespoon tomato paste
- 3 tablespoon tomato puree
- 3 teaspoon minced garlic
- 1 teaspoon paprika

DIRECTIONS

1. Firstly, make the marinade: chop Italian parsley and combine it with the paprika, minced garlic, olive oil, ground black pepper, tomato puree, and tomato paste in the big bowl.
2. Churn the mixture until you get the homogenous sauce.
3. Then chop the chicken breast into the medium cubes.
4. Put the chicken cubes in the sauce and coat the meat well.
5. Leave the chicken for 20 minutes to marinate.
6. After this, preheat the grill to 365 F.
7. Skewer the chicken cubes in the skewers and put them on the grill.
8. Grill the chicken kabobs for 7 minutes in total.
9. Enjoy the chicken kabobs with the grilled baguette.

ITALIAN CHICKEN DRUMSTICKS

PREPARATION
20 min

COOKING
35 min

SERVINGS
4

INGREDIENTS

- 1 cup ricotta
- ¼ cup olive oil
- 1 teaspoon salt
- 1-pound chicken drumsticks

DIRECTIONS

1. Whisk the ricotta with the olive oil and salt.
2. When you get a smooth and fluffy mass – the sauce is cooked.
3. Preheat the oven to 365 F.
4. Put the drumsticks in the ricotta sauce and mix the mixture well.
5. Then transfer the chicken mixture in the form and put the form in the preheated oven.
6. Cook the dish for 35 minutes. Stir it once during the cooking.
7. When the time is over – let the chicken for 10 minutes more in the oven.
8. After this, transfer the chicken to the serving plates.

ITALIAN CHICKEN NEAPOLITAN

PREPARATION
20 min

COOKING
60 min

SERVES
7

INGREDIENTS

- 2 oz leek
- 1 teaspoon dried parsley
- 4 tablespoon water
- 2 tablespoon cornstarch
- 1 cup chicken stock
- 1 teaspoon salt
- 1-pound chicken
- 10 oz artichokes, cooked
- 8 oz dried tomatoes
- 2 garlic clove
- 3 tablespoon olive oil
- 1 teaspoon ground black pepper

DIRECTIONS

1. Pour the olive oil into the big pan and preheat it.
2. The put the chicken in the hot olive oil and roast it carefully from all sides.
3. After this, remove the chicken from the pan.
4. Peel the garlic clove and slice it.
5. Chop the leek.
6. Add the prepared ingredients in the pan and cook them for 2 minutes more on the medium heat.
7. After this, sprinkle the chicken with the cooked vegetables and transfer it back to the pan.
8. Sprinkle the whole chicken with the dried parsley, salt, and ground black pepper.
9. Chop the tomatoes and artichokes and add them to the chicken.
10. Sprinkle the chicken with the chicken stock and close the lid.
11. Cook the dish on the medium heat for 45 minutes.
12. Then combine the water and cornstarch together. Whisk it until homogenous.
13. Cover the chicken with the cornstarch mixture and cook for 15 minutes more.
14. Let the cooked dish chill well.

RISOTTO

ORANGE RISOTTO

PREPARATION
15 min

COOKING
20 min

SERVINGS
4

INGREDIENTS

- 2 oranges, zest, juice
- 1 orange, cut into small pieces
- 2 tbsp. of olive oil
- 1 onion, chopped finely
- 2 carrots, grated
- 3 cups of risotto rice
- 2 ½ pints of boiling chicken stock
- ½ cup of white wine
- 1 tbsp. of butter
- Salt and pepper

DIRECTIONS

1. Heat the olive oil in a large saucepan.
2. Add and sweat the onion with the carrot until soft and tender but not colored.
3. Add the rice and cook for 2 to 3 minutes until the grain start to color slightly.
4. Add the orange juice and the wine, stirring constantly until the liquid is all absorbed.
5. Add the orange pieces.
6. Add the vegetable stock little by little, stirring constantly until the liquid is all absorbed before adding some more.
7. Add half of the orange zest and season. Mix well.
8. Add the butter and cook further for 1 minute.
9. Serve immediately and sprinkle the rest of the orange zest as a garnish.

FETA CHEESE AND MUSSELS RISOTTO

PREPARATION
15 min

COOKING
30 min

SERVINGS
4

INGREDIENTS

- ½ lb. of feta cheese, cut into small cubes
- ½ lb. of mascarpone
- 1 lb. of mussels, cooked
- 3 cups of risotto rice
- 3 shallots, chopped
- 4 tomatoes, cut into cubes
- ½ cup of white wine
- 1 cup of fish stock
- 5 tbsp. of olive oil
- 2 tbsp. of coriander
- Salt and pepper

DIRECTIONS

1. Warm up the olive oil in a large saucepan.
2. Add and sweat the shallots until soft and tender.
3. Add the rice and cook it until it becomes transparent. Stir constantly.
4. Pour the fish stock little by little into the rice. Reduce the heat to medium.
5. Cook the rice until complete absorption of the liquid stirring occasionally.
6. Add the feta cheese and the mascarpone.
7. Add the mussels and the coriander. Season.
8. Add the tomatoes and mix well everything together.
9. Serve immediately.

SCALLOPS RISOTTO

PREPARATION
15 min

COOKING
40 min

SERVES
4

INGREDIENTS

- 16 nuts of scallops
- 2 Tbsp. of olive oil
- 1 Tbsp. of curry
- 4 Tbsp. of coconut milk
- 2 limes, juiced
- 1 onion, chopped finely
- 3 cups of risotto rice
- 2 ½ pints of boiling fish broth
- 3 Tbsp. of grated parmesan
- Salt and pepper

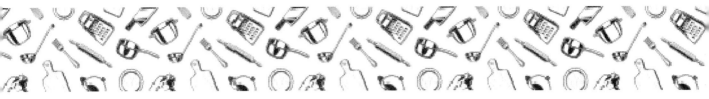

DIRECTIONS

1. Mix the hot fish broth with the curry powder.
2. Heat the olive oil in a large saucepan.
3. Add and sweat the onion until soft and tender but not colored.
4. Add the rice and cook for 2 to 3 minutes until the grain start to color slightly.
5. Add the fish curry broth little by little, stirring constantly until the liquid is all absorbed before adding some more.
6. Before you finish all the stock add the lime juice.
7. Add the rest of the vegetable stock.
8. Heat and melt the butter in a frying pan.
9. Add the scallops and fry 1 minute on each side.
10. Season and add the coconut milk cook for a further 2 minutes.
11. Meanwhile, sprinkle the parmesan in the risotto.
12. Give a good stir and cook for a further one minute.
13. Serve immediately and on each plate add four scallops with the coconut sauce.

DUCK RISOTTO

PREPARATION
15 min

COOKING
40 min

SERVES
4

INGREDIENTS

- 3 duck breasts
- 1 celery sticks, finely chopped
- 2 carrots, cut into cubes
- 1 onion, chopped finely
- 2 garlic cloves, crushed
- 1 sprig of thyme
- ½ cup of mushrooms
- 4 tbsp. of olive oil
- 3 cups of risotto rice
- 1 ½ pints of boiling chicken stock
- ½ cup of red wine
- 1 tbsp. of butter
- Salt and pepper

DIRECTIONS

1. Warm-up two Tbsp. of olive oil in a large frying pan.
2. Cook the duck breasts skin first for 3 to 4 minutes on each side.
3. Remove and slice the breasts and cover it to keep warm. Leave on the side.
4. Warm up the other two Tbsp. of olive oil in a large saucepan.
5. Add and sweat the onion and garlic until soft and tender but not colored.
6. Add the carrots, mushrooms, celery, and thyme. Cook for 2 minutes.
7. Add the rice and cook further for another 2 to 3 minutes until the grain starts to slightly color.
8. Add the red wine and stir constantly until the wine is completely absorbed by the rice.
9. Add the chicken stock little by little.
10. Stir constantly until the liquid is all absorbed before adding some more.
11. Add the butter and season. Mix well.
12. Serve and place the sliced duck on each plate and enjoy.

WHITE ASPARAGUS RISOTTO

PREPARATION
15 min

COOKING
50 min

SERVINGS
4

INGREDIENTS

- 1 lb. of white asparagus
- 3 cups of risotto rice
- 1 onion, chopped
- 1 garlic clove, chopped
- 1 tbsp. of sugar
- 1 lemon, juiced
- 1 tbsp. of white wine
- 3 tbsp. of butter
- 3 tbsp. of grated parmesan
- Salt and pepper

DIRECTIONS

1. Boil 1.5 pint of salted water in a large saucepan.
2. Add one Tbsp. of sugar and the lemon juice.
3. Add one Tbsp. of butter and the asparagus.
4. Boil for 10 minutes at low heat.
5. Drain and left aside. Keep 2 cups of the liquid.
6. Warm-up and melt the rest of the butter in a large saucepan.
7. Add and sweat the onion until soft and tender.
8. Add the rice and cook until it becomes transparent. Stir constantly.
9. Add the white wine.
10. Pour the leftover liquid little by little into the rice.
11. Cook the rice until complete absorption of the liquid and stir occasionally.
12. Just before the end of adding the liquid add the asparagus.
13. Add the parmesan and season. Mix well.
14. Serve immediately

GREEN RISOTTO

PREPARATION
15 min

COOKING
40 min

SERVINGS
4

INGREDIENTS

- 6 oz. green beans, cut in halves
- 6 oz. mange tout, cut in halves
- 6 oz. broccoli florets, cut into equal pieces
- 6 oz. zucchini, sliced
- 6 or of peas
- 1 onion, chopped finely
- 2 tbsp. of olive oil
- 3 cups of risotto rice
- 1 ½ pints of boiling vegetable stock
- ½ cup of white wine
- 1 tbsp. of butter
- 3 tbsp. of grated parmesan
- Salt and pepper

DIRECTIONS

1. Warm up the olive oil in a large saucepan.
2. Add and sweat the onion until soft and tender but not colored.
3. Add the rice and cook further for another 2 to 3 minutes until the grain starts to slightly color.
4. Add the mangetout, green beans, broccoli, and peas.
5. Add the white wine and stir constantly until the liquid is all absorbed.
6. Add the vegetable stock little by little. Stir constantly until the liquid is all absorbed before adding some more.
7. Add half of the parmesan and butter. Season and mix well.
8. Cook until the butter is melted and serve immediately.
9. Sprinkle the rest of the parmesan on each plate.

HAM AND PEAS RISOTTO

PREPARATION
15 min

COOKING
30 min

SERVINGS
4

INGREDIENTS

- 12 oz. of peas
- 2 tbsp. of butter
- 1 onion, chopped
- 2 garlic cloves, chopped
- 10 oz. of risotto rice
- ¼ pint of white wine
- 1 ¼ pint of vegetable stock
- 3 tbsp. of parmesan
- Salt and pepper

DIRECTIONS

1. Blanch the peas in boiling water for 2 to 3 minutes.
2. Drain and cool down under cold water and leave aside.
3. Heat the butter in a large saucepan.
4. Add and sweat the onion until soft.
5. Add the garlic and cook further for another2 minutes.
6. Add the rice and the wine and bring to the boiling stage.
7. Then reduce the heat and cook until the wine is absorbed.
8. Heat the vegetable stock separately.
9. Add a ladle of the stock at the time to the rice until it is absorbed by the rice.
10. Repeat until all the vegetable stock is gone.
11. Add the peas and ham with the last ladle. Season.
12. Sprinkle with the parmesan and serve immediately.

RISOTTO AI FRUTTI DI MARE

PREPARATION
15 min

COOKING
30 min

SERVINGS
4

INGREDIENTS

- 8 oz. of clams
- 8 oz. of mussels
- 4 oz. of shrimps
- 4 oz. of squids
- 2 tbsp. of olive oil
- 1 shallot, chopped finely
- 3 cups of risotto rice
- ½ white wine
- 1 pint of fish broth
- 3 Tbsp. of single cream
- Salt and pepper

DIRECTIONS

1. Warm up the olive oil in a large saucepan.
2. Add and sweat the shallot until soft and tender but not colored.
3. Add the rice and cook for 2 to 3 minutes until the grain starts to slightly color.
4. Add the fish broth little by little. Stir constantly until the liquid is all absorbed before adding some more.
5. Halfway through add the clams, mussels, shrimps, and squids.
6. Finish the rest of the fish broth the same way until the rice absorbs it all.
7. Add the cream and stir well and cook further for one more minute. Season.
8. Serve immediately.

FISH RISOTTO

PREPARATION
15 min

COOKING
50 min

SERVES
4

INGREDIENTS

- 2 salmon filets
- 2 cod fillets
- 1 leek, chopped finely
- ½ cup of peas
- 2 tbsp. of olive oil
- 1 shallot, chopped finely
- 1 garlic clove, chopped finely
- 3 cups of risotto rice
- ½ white wine
- 1 tbsp. of butter
- 1 tbsp. of dill
- 1 pint of fish broth
- Salt and pepper

DIRECTIONS

1. Warm up the olive oil in a large saucepan.
2. Add the fish filets and cook them thoroughly. Season.
3. Remove and crumble the filets into little pieces and leave on the side.
4. Add and sweat the shallot and garlic until soft and tender but not colored.
5. Add the leek and peas.
6. Add the rice and cook for 2 to 3 minutes until the grain starts to slightly color.
7. Add the white wine and stir constantly until the rice absorbed the wine.
8. Add the fish broth little by little. Stir constantly until the liquid is all absorbed before adding some more.
9. Halfway through add the crumbled fish back to it.
10. Finish the rest of the fish broth the same way until the rice absorbs it all.
11. Add the butter and the dill and cook further for one more minute. Season to your taste.
12. Serve immediately.

PUMPKIN RISOTTO

PREPARATION
15 min

COOKING
40 min

SERVINGS
4

INGREDIENTS

- 16 oz. of pumpkin, cut into small cubes
- 3 cups of risotto rice
- 1 onion, chopped
- 4 tbsp. of olive oil
- 1 cups of vegetable broth
- 3 tbsp. of grated parmesan
- 1 Tbsp. of coriander
- 1 tbsp. of butter

DIRECTIONS

1. Warm up the olive oil in a large saucepan.
2. Add and sweat the onion until soft and tender.
3. Add the pumpkin and cook for 2 to 3 minutes by stirring constantly.
4. Add the rice and cook until it becomes transparent. Stir constantly.
5. Heat the vegetable broth separately and bring to the boiling stage.
6. Pour the broth little by little into the rice. Make sure it is always boiling. Reduce the heat to low.
7. Cook the rice until complete absorption of the liquid and stir occasionally.
8. Add the parmesan and butter and season. Mix well.
9. Sprinkle the risotto of coriander and serve immediately.

MILANESE RISOTTO

PREPARATION
15 min

COOKING
30 min

SERVINGS
4

INGREDIENTS

- 2 good pinches of saffron threads
- 3 tbsp. of butter
- 1 onion, chopped finely
- 2 garlic cloves, crushed
- 3 cups of risotto rice
- 1 cup of white wine
- 2 pints of boiling vegetable stock
- 3 tbsp. of grated parmesan
- Salt and pepper

DIRECTIONS

1. Put the saffron into a small bowl.
2. Cover it with 4 Tbsp. of vegetable stock and leave to soak until needed.
3. Heat and melt 2 Tbsp. of butter in a large saucepan.
4. Add and sweat the onion and garlic until soft and tender but not colored.
5. Add the rice and cook for 2 to 3 minutes until the grain start to color slightly.
6. Add the white wine stirring from time to time until it is all absorbed.
7. Add the vegetable stock little by little. Stir constantly until the liquid is all absorbed before adding some more.
8. Add the saffron liquid with the rest of the butter.
9. Add the parmesan and season. Mix well.
10. Cover the pan tightly and leave to stand for 5 minutes off the heat.
11. Give a good stir and serve immediately.

FISH

LINGUINE AND SHRIMP SCAMPI

PREPARATION
15 min

COOKING
30 min

SERVINGS
4

INGREDIENTS

- 1 package linguine pasta
- ¼ cup butter
- 1 chopped red bell pepper
- 5 minced garlic cloves
- 45 raw large shrimp peeled and deveined
- ½ cup dry white wine
- ¼ cup chicken broth
- 2 tbsp. lemon juice
- ¼ cup of butter
- 1 tsp. crushed red pepper flakes
- ½ tsp. saffron
- ¼ cup chopped parsley
- Salt to taste

DIRECTIONS

1. Prepare the pasta according to directions, about 10 minutes.
2. Drain and set aside.
3. Melt the butter in a large skillet.
4. Sauté the bell pepper and garlic for 5 minutes.
5. Stir in the shrimp and sauté for another 5 minutes.
6. Transfer the shrimp to a plate but keep the pepper and garlic in the skillet.
7. Add the white wine, broth, and lemon juice and bring to a boil.
8. Add another ¼ cup of better and transfer the shrimp back to the skillet.
9. Stir in the red pepper flakes, saffron, and parsley, and season with salt as needed.
10. Toss with the pasta and simmer for 5 minutes.

BAKED HALIBUT

PREPARATION
15 min

COOKING
30 min

SERVINGS
4

INGREDIENTS

- 1 teaspoon olive oil
- 1 cup zucchini, chopped
- 1 cup onion, minced
- 2 cloves garlic, crushed and minced
- 2 cups tomatoes, diced
- 2 tablespoons fresh basil leaves, chopped
- Salt and pepper to taste
- ¼ teaspoon salt
- 4 halibut steaks
- ¼ cup feta cheese, crumbled

DIRECTIONS

1. Preheat your oven to 450 degrees F.
2. Pour the oil into a pan over medium heat.
3. Cook the onion, garlic, and zucchini for 5 minutes.
4. Stir in the salt, pepper, basil, and tomatoes.
5. Place the fish steaks in a baking pan.
6. Top the fish with the zucchini mixture.
7. Sprinkle the feta cheese on top.
8. Bake in the oven for 15 minutes.

LOBSTER FRA DIAVOLO

PREPARATION
15 min

COOKING
42 min

SERVES
4

INGREDIENTS

- 3 tbsp. virgin olive oil
- 2 garlic cloves (finely chopped)
- 1 medium onion (peeled, finely chopped)
- 1 cup Italian dry white wine
- 3 cups chopped, canned Italian tomato
- 2 tbsp. fresh basil (finely chopped)
- Red pepper flakes
- 2 (1½ pound) lobsters
- 1-pound fresh linguine
- 3 tbsp. finely chopped parsley

DIRECTIONS

1. In a large saucepan, heat the oil.
2. Add onions to the pan and cook till onions turn translucent and softened, next add the chopped garlic.
3. Cook the garlic for 60-90 seconds, or until it emits its fragrance.
4. Add the dry white wine and cook until the liquid reduces by half.
5. Next, add the canned tomatoes and stir to combine.
6. Season according to taste. Sprinkle in the fresh basil and add a dash of red pepper flakes.
7. Cook for 12-15 minutes over a low heat.
8. Cut each of the lobster in half, across their length, and add to the sauce.
9. Cook for 15-20 minutes on low, until bright pink and the lobster meat is sufficiently cooked.
10. Remove the lobster from the sauce and cut the lobster meat from the claws and the tail and cut into bite-sized pieces.
11. Return the lobster meat to the sauce and keep warm.
12. In the meantime, and while the lobster is cooking, add salted water to a pot and bring to boil.
13. Add pasta and cook al dente.
14. Drain return it to the pot.
15. Add 2-3 ladles of sauce to the linguine and over moderate heat, stir well to combine.
16. Evenly divide the linguine into 4 pasta bowls and top with the remaining sauce.
17. Sprinkle parsley over the top and serve.

SHRIMP ALFREDO

PREPARATION
15 min

COOKING
40 min

SERVINGS
4

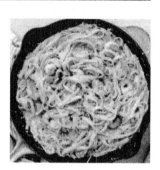

INGREDIENTS

- 2 tablespoons olive oil
- ¼ cup butter
- 1 onion, diced
- 2 cloves garlic, minced
- ½ lb. Portobello mushrooms, sliced
- 1 red bell pepper, chopped
- 1 lb. shrimp, shelled and deveined
- 15 oz. Alfredo sauce
- ½ cup Romano cheese, grated
- ½ cup cream
- Pinch cayenne pepper
- Salt and pepper to taste
- 12 oz. penne pasta, cooked according to package directions

DIRECTIONS

1. Add the olive oil and butter to a pan over medium heat.
2. Cook the onion and garlic for 2 to 3 minutes, stirring often.
3. Add the mushrooms and red bell pepper.
4. Cook for 2 minutes.
5. Add the shrimp.
6. Pour in the cream and Alfredo sauce.
7. Stir in the cheese.
8. Simmer for 5 minutes or until the sauce has thickened.
9. Season with the salt, pepper, and cayenne.
10. Toss the pasta in the sauce and top with the parsley.

LOBSTER RAVIOLI

PREPARATION
15 min

COOKING
45 min

SERVINGS
4

INGREDIENTS

- 2 pounds fresh uncooked lobster meat
- 2 bunches leeks
- 1/2 bunch fresh parsley
- Fresh-cracked black pepper
- 1 recipe classic pasta dough, uncut and uncooked

DIRECTIONS

1. Roughly chop lobster meat into bite-sized pieces. Thoroughly wash and dry the leeks. Thinly slice. Clean and chop the parsley.
2. In a large bowl, combine lobster, leeks, parsley, and black pepper.
3. Roll out pasta onto a floured surface into sheets about 1/2 inch thick. Cut into circles 3 inches in diameter.
4. Bring 2 gallons of water to a slow boil. Then add in ravioli and cook until al dente, approximately 10 minutes.
5. Serve the ravioli with the sauce of your choice and sprinkle with black pepper.

SALMON PESTO

PREPARATION
15 min

COOKING
40 min

SERVINGS
4

INGREDIENTS

- 2 lb. salmon fillets
- 1 tablespoon lemon juice
- 1 lemon, sliced
- 1 ½ cups pesto
- ½ cup white wine

DIRECTIONS

1. Grease your baking pan with oil.
2. Add the salmon to the baking pan.
3. Pour the wine over the fish and drizzle with the lemon juice.
4. Marinate for 15 minutes.
5. Preheat your broiler.
6. Spread the pesto on top of the fish.
7. Broil the fish for 10 minutes.
8. Add the lemon slices on top of the fish.
9. Broil for another 5 minutes.

COD WITH TOPPING

PREPARATION
15 min

COOKING
40 min

SERVINGS
4

INGREDIENTS

- 4 cod fillets
- ¼ cup buttermilk
- ¼ cup unflavored Panko breadcrumbs
- 3 tbsp. grated Parmigiano Reggiano
- 2 tbsp. cornmeal
- 1 tbsp. olive oil
- ¼ tsp. basil
- ¼ tsp. oregano
- Salt and pepper to taste – easy on the salt
- 2 minced garlic cloves
- 3 tbsp. mayonnaise
- 1 tsp. lemon juice

DIRECTIONS

1. Soak the cod in the buttermilk for 1 hour.
2. Preheat the oven to 450 degrees 3. Combine the Panko, cheese, cornmeal, olive oil, basil, oregano, salt, and pepper in a bowl.
3. Lightly butter a broiler pan.
4. Transfer the cod into the broiler pan.
5. Combine the garlic, mayonnaise, and lemon juice in a bowl.
6. Coat the cod with the mayonnaise mixture, then top with the Panko mixture.
7. Bake for 10 minutes.

SHRIMP WITH PESTO CREAM SAUCE

PREPARATION
15 min

COOKING
10 min

SERVINGS
4

INGREDIENTS

- 1 package linguine pasta
- 1 tbsp. olive oil
- 1 chopped onion
- 1 cup sliced mushrooms
- 6 minced garlic cloves
- ½ cup butter
- Salt and pepper to taste
- ½ tsp. cayenne pepper
- 1 3/4 cups grated Pecorino Romano
- 3 tbsp. flour
- ½ cup heavy cream
- 1 cup pesto
- 1 lb. cooked shrimp, peeled and deveined

DIRECTIONS

1. Prepare the pasta according to directions, about 10 minutes. Drain.
2. Heat the oil in a skillet and sauté the onion and mushrooms for 5 minutes
3. Stir in the garlic and butter and cook for 1 minute.
4. Add the heavy cream to the skillet and season with salt, pepper, and cayenne pepper.
5. Next, simmer for 5 minutes.
6. Stir in the cheese. Keep stirring until the cheese is melted.
7. Then, stir in the flour to thicken the sauce.
8. Add the pesto and shrimp and cook for 5 minutes.
9. Toss with the pasta to coat.

DESSERTS

TIRAMISU-NEW

PREPARATION
20 min

COOKING
40 min

SERVINGS
8

INGREDIENTS

- 7 tablespoon mascarpone
- 10 oz ladyfingers
- ¼ cup brewed coffee
- 2 teaspoon cocoa powder
- 5 egg yolks
- 6 tablespoon sugar
- 1 teaspoon vanilla extract

DIRECTIONS

1. Whisk the yolks with the sugar until you get a lemon color mixture.
2. After this, add vanilla extract and mascarpone.
3. Continue to whisk the mixture for 1 minute more.
4. Then make the layer of the ladyfingers.
5. Sprinkle the ladyfingers with the brewed coffee.
6. Then make the layer of the whisked mascarpone cream and cover it with the ladyfingers again.
7. Add the second layer of the mascarpone cream.
8. Sprinkle the tiramisu with the cocoa powder.
9. Put the cooked tiramisu in the fridge for 5 hours to make the ladyfinger to soak the mascarpone cream.

ALMOND ITALIAN COOKIES

PREPARATION
10 min

COOKING
25 min

SERVINGS
8

INGREDIENTS

- 1 cup almond flakes
- 5 eggs
- 4 tablespoon strawberry jam
- 1 teaspoon vanilla extract
- ¼ teaspoon almond extract
- 2 cup almond flour
- ½ cup sugar
- ¼ teaspoon salt

DIRECTIONS

1. Beat 4 eggs in the mixer bowl and whisk them.
2. Add almond flour and strawberry jam.
3. After this, add salt and vanilla extract.
4. Knead the non-sticky dough.
5. Whisk the egg in the bowl.
6. Make the log from the almond flour dough and cut it into the small balls.
7. Then deep the almond flour balls in the whisked egg.
8. After this, coat the almond flour balls in the almond flakes.
9. Preheat the oven to 365 F.
10. Put the cookies on the tray and cook them for 25 minutes.
11. Then chill the cookies very well.
12. Serve the dish immediately.

SICILIAN CANNOLI

PREPARATION
10 min

COOKING
13 min

SERVES
9

INGREDIENTS

- 5 teaspoon red wine
- 4 teaspoon butter
- 1 egg
- 1 cup olive oil
- 8 oz ricotta
- 1 cup flour
- 2 teaspoon sugar
- 4 teaspoon cocoa powder
- 1/3 teaspoon wine vinegar
- 1 cup white sugar
- ¼ teaspoon vanilla extract
- 2 tablespoon orange zest

DIRECTIONS

1. Sift the flour into the bowl.
2. Add sugar and cocoa powder.
3. After this, add wine vinegar and butter.
4. Beat the egg in the mixture and knead the smooth and non-sticky dough.
5. Then roll the dough into the thin circle.
6. Make the circles from the dough with the help of the cutter.
7. Pour olive oil into the saucepan and make it hot.
8. Sprinkle the cannoli from with the oil gently and wrap the dough circles on the cannoli forms.
9. After this, put the cannoli with the forms in the hot oil and fry it for 1 minute or until the cannoli is golden brown.
10. Chill the cooked cannoli and dry them with the help of the paper towel.
11. Make the filling for the cannoli: combine ricotta and white sugar in the mixer bowl.
12. Add vanilla extract and mix it carefully with the help of the mixer.
13. After this, put the ricotta cream in the pastry bag and fill the cannoli.
14. Sprinkle the dessert with the orange zest.

PANNA COTTA

PREPARATION
10 min

COOKING
10 min

SERVES
4

INGREDIENTS

- 6 tablespoon white sugar
- 1 teaspoon vanilla extract
- 1 teaspoon fresh mint
- 5 tablespoon milk
- ½ cup heavy cream
- 1 tablespoon gelatin

DIRECTIONS

1. Combine gelatin with the milk and whisk it until gelatin is dissolved.
2. After this, pour the heavy cream into the saucepan and preheat it.
3. When the heavy cream is hot – add vanilla extract and gelatin mixture very slowly.
4. Whisk it constantly till the gelatin and heavy cream mixture are combined.
5. Then add sugar and continue to whisk the creamy mixture until sugar is dissolved.
6. Then remove the cooked creamy mixture from the heat and chill it well.
7. Pour the ice water into the bowl and put the saucepan with the cream mixture there.
8. Whisk it carefully to get the warm mixture.
9. Then pour the panna cotta in the serving glasses and the dessert in the fridge.
10. Refrigerate the panna cotta until it is solid.
11. Then put the fresh mint on the top of the panna cotta.

YOGURT MOUSSE

PREPARATION
8 min

COOKING
3 min

SERVINGS
4

INGREDIENTS

- 2 tablespoons water
- For the berries:
- 1 tablespoon honey
- ¼ cup balsamic vinegar
- A pinch of black pepper
- 2 cups yogurt
- ¼ cup honey
- A pinch of salt
- ½ vanilla bean
- ¾ cup heavy cream
- 2 cups mixed blueberries and raspberries
- 4 amaretto cookies, crushed

DIRECTIONS

1. Strain yogurt, spoon into a cheesecloth, press, cover, and keep in the fridge for 4 hours.
2. Heat up a pan with the water and a pinch of salt over medium-high heat, add ¼ cup honey, vanilla seeds, and the bean, stir, bring to a boil, cook for 2 minutes, take off heat, leave aside to cool down for 10 minutes and discard vanilla bean.
3. Mix cream with a mixer, add yogurt and whisk for 3 minutes.
4. Divide this into dessert glasses, cover and keep in the fridge for 4 hours.
5. Before serving the mousse, heat up a pan over medium heat, add vinegar, a pinch of pepper, and 1 tablespoon honey, stir, bring to a boil and simmer for 2 minutes.
6. Take off heat, add berries, stir and pour over yogurt mousse.
7. Garnish each glass with crumbled amaretto cookies.

ITALIAN WEDDING COOKIES

PREPARATION
20 min

COOKING
80 min

SERVINGS
40

INGREDIENTS

- 3 cups all-purpose flour, sifted
- ¾ cup confectioners' sugar
- 4 ½ teaspoons vanilla extract
- 1 ½ cups almonds, finely ground
- ⅓ cup confectioners' sugar for rolling
- 1 ½ cups butter, unsalted
- ¾ teaspoon salt

DIRECTIONS

1. Preheat your oven to 325 F.
2. Cream margarine or butter in a large bowl, slowly add the salt and confectioners' sugar.
3. Beat until light & fluffy. Add vanilla and almonds.
4. Slowly, blend the flour; mix well.
5. Shape into crescents or balls using approximately 1 teaspoon for each cookie.
6. Arrange them on cookie sheets (ungreased) and bake in the preheated oven for 15 to 20 minutes. Don't let them brown.
7. Let them cool slightly and then roll in the additional confectioners' sugar.

ITALIAN CHRISTMAS COOKIES

PREPARATION
50 min

COOKING
155 min

SERVES
54

INGREDIENTS

For Cookies:
- 2 ½ cups all-purpose flour
- 1 ¼ cups granulated sugar
- 2 teaspoons lemon peel, grated
- ½ cup butter, softened
- 2 teaspoons baking powder
- ⅓ cup whole milk ricotta cheese
- 2 eggs, large
- 1 teaspoon vanilla
- ½ teaspoon salt

For Frosting:
- 3 to 4 tablespoons lemon juice, fresh
- Candy sprinkles, as desired
- 2 ¼ cups powdered sugar
- Food colors, as desired

DIRECTIONS

1. Preheat your oven to 350 F.
2. Stir flour together with salt and baking powder in a small-sized bowl.
3. Beat the granulated sugar together with ricotta cheese, softened butter & lemon peel on medium speed using an electric mixer in a large bowl, for a minute or so, until fluffy; scraping the side of the bowl, as required.
4. Slowly beat in the eggs until just smooth.
5. Add the vanilla; give everything a good stir.
6. Beat the flour mixture into the sugar mixture at low speed until blended well.
7. Cover & refrigerate for half an hour.
8. Shape the dough into 1" (54) balls using floured fingers; arrange them on ungreased cookie sheets, 2" apart.
9. Bake in the preheated oven until set but not brown, for 9 to 11 minutes.
10. Let them cool for a minute or two and then remove from cookie sheets.
11. Transfer them on a cooling rack to completely cool.
12. Using a large wooden spoon, beat the powdered sugar together with 3 tablespoons of lemon juice in a small-sized bowl until smooth & spreadable.
13. Add more lemon juice if the frosting is too stiff to spread.
14. Tint with food color and then spread ½ teaspoon of the frosting on each cooled cookie using a sharp knife, immediately top with sprinkles.
15. Let stand until the frosting is set, for half an hour.
16. Cover and store them in an airtight container.

ITALIAN FIG COOKIES

PREPARATION
10 min

COOKING
130 min

SERVES
36

INGREDIENTS

For Cookie Dough:

- 1 ½ tablespoons baking powder
- 4 cups all-purpose flour, unbleached
- 1 egg, large
- ½ cup sugar
- 1 cup vegetable shortening
- ½ cup milk
- 1 tablespoon pure vanilla extract
- ¼ teaspoon salt

For Filling:

- ¾ cup raisins
- 1 cup dates, dried, pitted
- ¼ cup honey
- 1 cup fig, dried
- ½ cup walnuts, chopped
- ¼ cup orange marmalade
- ½ teaspoon cinnamon

For Icing:

- 2 cups confectioners' sugar
- Colored sprinkles
- Milk or water

DIRECTIONS

For Cookie Dough:

1. Sift flour together with salt & baking powder in a large bowl.
2. Add sugar; give everything a good stir.
3. Using a pastry blender or fork; cut in the shortening & work the mixture until you get corn meal-like consistency.
4. Beat egg together with milk & vanilla in a bowl.
5. Add egg mixture to the flour mixture; using an electric mixer, mix until blended well and you get a soft dough, for a couple of minutes.
6. Divide the dough into 4 pieces & wrap each piece with a plastic wrap; let refrigerate for 40 to 45 minutes.

For Filling:

1. Grind the dates, figs & raisins together in a food processor until coarsely chopped and then place the chopped raisins, figs, and dates in a bowl.
2. Add the leftover filling ingredients; mix well until you get a thick mixture; set the mixture aside.
3. Preheat your oven to 375 F.
4. Work in batches and place the dough on a floured surface; roll the dough to a 12" square.

5. Cut the dough into 2x3" rectangles.
6. Spoon approximately 1 teaspoon of the filling on each rectangle.
7. Fold the long edges carefully over to meet in the center and pinch to seal the seam.
8. Place each cookie on a baking sheet, seam side down; ensure you leave a minimum space of 1" among the cookies.
9. Using a sharp knife; make 2 or 3 diagonal slits over each cookie.
10. Bake until the cookies are golden in color, for 12 to 15 minutes.
11. Remove from the oven and transfer the cookies on a wire rack to completely cool.

For Icing:

1. Place the confectioner's sugar in a large bowl.
2. Add just a small amount of milk or water, until you get a smooth consistency.
3. Ice the tops of each cookie and then sprinkle with colored sprinkles.
4. Before stacking, let the icing to completely dry.
5. Store them in airtight containers for up to 2 weeks.

MERINGATA CHOCOLATE CHIP

PREPARATION
20 min

COOKING
95 min

SERVES
8

INGREDIENTS

- 6 egg whites, large, at room temperature
- ¼ cup confectioners' sugar
- 1-pound bittersweet chocolate, chopped finely
- ½ teaspoon pure vanilla extract
- 2 ¼ cups heavy cream
- ½ teaspoon cream of tartar
- 1 ½ cups granulated sugar
- ¼ cup hot brewed espresso

DIRECTIONS

1. Preheat your oven to 225 F in advance and position the racks in the lower & middle thirds of your oven. T

2. race an 11" circle on the undersides of 2 parchment paper sheets.

3. Line the baking sheets with these papers.

4. Beat egg whites with the cream of tartar in the bowl of a standing electric mixer attached with the whisk until foamy, at medium speed.

5. Increase the speed of your electric mixer to high & beat until soft peaks form.

6. Slowly add the granulated sugar; beat well after each addition.

7. Add the vanilla; beat for a couple of more minutes, until the whites are stiff & glossy.

8. Transfer half of the meringue to a pastry bag attached with a ½" plain round tip, piping a ring of meringue inside each drawn circle. Spoon the leftover meringue into the circles, spread it ½" thick. Bake in the preheated oven until very pale but dry, for 1 ½ hours.

9. Turn the oven off, slightly prop the door open and let the meringues cool until dry & crisp, for several hours in the oven.

10. Beat the confectioners' sugar with 2 cups of cream until firm using an electric mixer in a bowl.

11. Fold in ¼ of the chocolate.

12. Spread the cream over 1 round, spreading it to the edge.

13. Top with the second round and pressing it lightly. Freeze for a couple of hours, until the cream is firm.

14. In the meantime, melt the leftover chocolate in a bowl set over a pan of simmering water.

15. Turn the heat off, whisk in the leftover cream & espresso.

16. Cut the frozen cake into wedges using a serrated knife and transfer them to plates.

17. Let stand for a couple of minutes.

18. Spoon some of the sauce on each wedge. Serve & enjoy.

LA ROCCIATA

PREPARATION
10 min

COOKING
55 min

SERVES
12

INGREDIENTS

- 2 cups flour
- ½ cup golden raisins
- 4 egg yolks, large
- ¼ cup sugar
- 4 tablespoons butter, cold, unsalted & cut into small pieces
- 1 teaspoon cinnamon
- 2 green apples, peeled, cored & chopped
- 1 cup walnuts, chopped
- ¼ cup sugar
- 2 tablespoons white wine, dry
- ¼ cut pine nuts
- 2 tablespoons Sambuca, brandy or anisette
- 1 beaten egg, large
- ¼ cup extra virgin olive oil
- A pinch of salt

DIRECTIONS

1. Mix wine & oil in a large-sized bowl
2. Add flour together with salt & sugar in a food processor and pulse on high settings until evenly combined.
3. Slowly add the egg yolks, pulse again.
4. Add butter.
5. Pulse again until in tiny pieces.
6. With the motor still running, add oil; mix until you get a dough-like consistency.
7. Turn the dough out & knead until smooth, for a couple of minutes; feel free to add a small amount of more flour, if required.
8. Using plastic wrap; cover the dough & refrigerate for an hour
9. In the meantime, preheat your oven to 350 F.
10. Now, in a large bowl; toss apples together with raisins, sugar, nuts, liquor & spices.
11. Evenly divide the dough into four pieces.
12. Roll the dough between parchments to form 4 rectangles (12x8).
13. Refrigerate for several minutes.
14. Place the dough back to a lightly floured clean surface.
15. Spoon a cup of the apple filling on top of each rectangle approximately ½" up from along the edge, in a thick stripe.
16. Roll the pastry up to enclose the filling, pressing the seams to seal.
17. Transfer the rolls (seam sides down) to a large-sized cookie sheet & brush the tops with the beaten egg.
18. Bake in the preheated oven for 35 to 40 minutes, until golden brown.
19. Cut into chunks or in half & serve warm.

PANDORO

PREPARATION
12 hours

COOKING
55 min

SERVES
6

INGREDIENTS

For Biga:
- 1 ½ cups all-purpose flour, unbleached
- ⅛ teaspoon instant yeast
- ½ cup cool water

For Dough:
- ½ cup dried apricots, diced
- 2 cups unbleached all-purpose flour; or 1 cup unbleached all-purpose flour & 1 cup Italian-style flour and
- ¼ cup unsalted butter [4 tablespoons]
- 2 tablespoons water
- ½ cup golden raisins
- 1 tablespoon instant yeast
- ⅓ cup sugar
- 2 eggs, large
- ½ teaspoon Fiori di Sicilia
- 1 ½ teaspoons salt

DIRECTIONS

For Biga:

1. Combine flour together with yeast and water.
2. Mix until VERY stiff and fairly smooth.
3. Cover with a plastic wrap & let rest for overnight.

For Dough:

1. The following day, add the entire dough ingredients together (except the fruit) to the biga; mix & then knead; by mixer, clean hand, or bread machine; until you get a soft, smooth, dough-like consistency.
2. Let the dough to rise for an hour, covered.
3. Now, knead the fruit into the dough; try leaving most of it inside; don't let any fruit to come upon the surface as it would tend to burn the loaf.
4. Round the dough into a ball & then transfer it to a pandoro pan, lightly greased.
5. Cover & let rise for 2 hours, until puffy.
6. During the last 5 to 10 minutes, preheat your oven to 350 F.
7. Bake the bread in the preheated oven for 8 to 10 minutes.
8. Tent it lightly with an aluminum foil & bake until an instant-read thermometer reads 190 F, for 35 to 40 more minutes.
9. Remove & let rest for a couple of minutes, then gently remove it from the pan.
10. When cool, sprinkle the bread with non-melting white sugar or confectioners' sugar; slice and serve it with mascarpone cheese.

PANFORTE

PREPARATION
4 hours

COOKING
55 min

SERVES
6

INGREDIENTS

- 1 cup soft raisins [8 oz]
- 4 teaspoons Dutch-process cocoa powder, unsweetened plus more for dusting
- ⅛ teaspoon ground cloves
- ⅔ cup all-purpose flour
- 1 teaspoon ground cinnamon
- ½ teaspoon ground ginger
- ¾ cup sugar
- 1 cup whole hazelnuts, toasted & loose skins rubbed off with a kitchen towel
- ⅔ cup honey
- 1 cup whole almonds, toasted
- ¼ teaspoon salt

DIRECTIONS

1. Preheat your oven to 300 F.
2. Line a springform pan with parchment, using a round for bottom and a strip for the side.
3. Butter the paper well & then dust it with the cocoa powder, knocking any excess out.
4. Whisk flour together with spices, 4 teaspoons cocoa & salt in a large bowl; whisk well and then stir in the fruit and nuts.
5. Bring honey and sugar to a boil over moderate heat in a 2-quart heavy saucepan; stirring frequently until the sugar is completely dissolved, then boil for a couple of more minutes, until the thermometer reads 238 to 240 F, don't stir this time.
6. Immediately pour honey on top of the fruit mixture & quickly stir until well combined.
7. Quickly spoon the mixture into a springform pan, evenly spreading with the back of a spoon.
8. Dampen your hands and press mixture evenly and firmly into the pan to compact as much as possible.
9. Bake in the middle rack of your oven for 50 to 55 minutes, until edges begin to rise slightly & become matte.
10. Cool the panforte in pan on a rack completely and then remove the side of the pan; invert, peel the paper off.
11. Using a serrated knife; cut into small pieces.
12. Serve & enjoy.

GRILLED PEACHES

PREPARATION
10 min

COOKING
5 min

SERVINGS
4

INGREDIENTS

- 2 teaspoons salt
- 3 tablespoons sesame seeds, toasted
- 1 teaspoon mint
- 1 teaspoon nigella seeds
- ½ teaspoon marjoram, dried
- 1/3 cup almonds, toasted
- 1/3 cup pistachios, toasted
- 1 tablespoon cumin seeds
- 1 tablespoon caraway seeds
- 1 tablespoon cumin seeds
- 1 teaspoon crushed pepper
- 1 teaspoon lemon zest, grated
- 4 peaches, halved
- A drizzle of olive oil
- Whipped cream
- Blueberries

DIRECTIONS

1. In your food processor, mix pistachios with almonds, coriander, cumin, caraway, crushed pepper, sesame seeds, salt, nigella seeds, mint, marjoram, and lemon zest and ground everything well.

2. Heat up your grill over medium-high heat, add peach halves, brush them with some oil, grill for 4 minutes, and divide between plates.

3. Add some of the nuts mix you've made and serve with blueberries and whipped cream.

ALMOND CAKE

PREPARATION
10 min

COOKING
40 min

SERVINGS
10

INGREDIENTS

- Zest from 1 orange, grated
- 1 and ¼ cups sugar
- 6 eggs, whites, and yolks separated
- ½ pound almonds, blanched and ground
- Zest from 1 lemon, grated
- 4 drops almond extract
- Confectioner's sugar

DIRECTIONS

1. Beat egg yolks with your mixer very well.
2. Add sugar, almond extract, orange, and lemon zest and almonds and stir well.
3. Beat egg whites in another bowl with your mixer.
4. Add egg yolks mix and stir everything.
5. Pour this into a greased baking dish, introduce in the oven at 350 degrees F and bake for 40 minutes.
6. Take the cake out of the oven, leave it to cool down, slice, dust confectioners' sugar on top, and serve.

ORANGE AND HAZELNUT CAKE

PREPARATION
10 min

COOKING
40 min

SERVES
10

INGREDIENTS

For the syrup:
- 2 and ½ tablespoons orange juice
- 1 and ¼ cups sugar
- 2/3 cup water
- 2 and ½ tablespoons orange water
- Zest from 1 orange, grated

For the cake:
- 2 and ¼ cups hazelnut flour
- 5 eggs, whites, and yolks separated
- 1 cup sugar
- 2 tablespoons confectioners' sugar for serving
- 1 and 1/3 cups Greek yogurt for serving
- Pulp from 4 passion fruits

DIRECTIONS

1. Put the water in a pot and bring to a boil over medium-high heat.
2. Add orange juice and 1 and ¼ cups sugar, stir and boil for 10 minutes.
3. Take off heat, add orange zest and orange water, stir and leave aside.
4. In a bowl, beat egg yolks with 1 cup sugar and hazelnut flour using your mixer.
5. In another bowl, beat egg whites using your mixer as well.
6. Combine the 2 mixtures and stir well.
7. Pour this batter into a greased and lined baking form, introduce in the oven at 350 degrees F, and bake for 30 minutes.
8. Take the cake out of the oven, leave it to cool down a bit, slice and serve with the orange sauce you've made, with yogurt, confectioners' sugar dusted on top, and passion fruit pulp on the side.

ESPRESSO PEANUT BUTTER BROWNIES

PREPARATION
15 min

COOKING
35 min

SERVINGS
4

INGREDIENTS

- 1 egg
- 1/3 cup of vegetable oil
- ¼ teaspoon of salt
- ¾ cup of peanut butter chips
- 2 tablespoons of espresso powder
- 18 Oz of brownie mix

DIRECTIONS

1. Preheat the oven to 350 F.
2. In a bowl, whisk 1/3 cup of water, oil, egg, and espresso powder.
3. Stir the brownie mix in until it blends well.
4. Stir in the peanut butter chips, transfer the batter into a prepared baking pan.
5. Sprinkle with salt evenly and bake for 33-37 minutes.
6. Cut into squares and serve.

ALMOND AND CHERRY COOKIES

PREPARATION
16 min

COOKING
30 min

SERVINGS
4

INGREDIENTS

- 2 tablespoons of limoncello
- 1 egg
- 4 cups of almond flour
- ¼ cup of honey
- ½ cup of sugar
- ¼ teaspoon of salt
- 3 tablespoons of cherry jam
- 1 teaspoon of lemon zest

DIRECTIONS

1. Preheat the oven to 350 F.
2. Spread 2 cups of almond flour on a rimmed baking sheet.
3. Place in the oven for 15 minutes and stir after 7-9 minutes until brown and toasted.
4. Cool the flour in a bowl, add the remaining flour, honey, sugar, lemon zest, salt, egg, and limoncello and combine to form a dough.
5. Scoop tablespoon-sized heaping scoops into a prepared baking sheet, flatten slightly, and make a small indent on each cookie.
6. Fill each cookie with ½ teaspoon of cherry jam and bake for 14-17 minutes.
7. Allow to cool and serve.

CONCLUSION

It's so easy to fall in love with Italian cuisine. From pasta to pizza and everything in between, you'd surely find Italian dishes worth the time and effort.

Thanks to this book, you don't have to take a trip to Italy or dine in fancy Italian restaurants to get a taste of delicious and authentic Italian dishes.

You now know what the basic parts of each homemade Italian dish, how to make them, and how to assemble your very own gustatory masterpiece.

But as knowledge is only half the battle, the things you learned in this book is just, well, half the meals. To make it whole, you'll need to actually try them out.

I sincerely hope that the book has succeeded in its mission to stop depending on commercial foods and prepare them at home with easy to follow instructions.

Happy cooking.

Printed in Great Britain
by Amazon

71148162R00115